Contents

Guidelines

for SCIENTIFIC

PUBLISHING

ICSU Press
Committee on Dissemination
of Scientific Information

Published by the International Council for Science (ICSU)
51 Boulevard de Montmorency, 75016 Paris, France.

© copyright ICSU 1988, 1994, 1999

First published in 1988 under the title
Guidelines for Printing and Publishing
Third edition 1999

Printed and bound in Great Britain by
Lindsay Ross International Ltd,
London and Oxford

ISBN: 0-930357-44-2.

An electronic version is available and may be accessed online at the
following URL:http://associnst.ox.ac.uk/~icsuinfo/guidelines.htm

6

PREFACE

This third edition of *Guidelines to Scientific Publishing* was prepared under contract by Anthony Watkinson following a decision of the ICSU Committee on the dissemination of Scientific Information.
The contract was supervised by a Steering Committee whose membership comprised:

> Glyn Jones
> Sally Morris
> Dennis Shaw (chairman & editor)
> Roger Elliott (corresponding)
> Howard Moore (corresponding)

As with former editions, these guidelines should be taken both as an attempt to help and advise the ICSU family and as an invitation to them, and others reading the compilation, to share their experiences with ICSU Press for the benefit of fellow scientists. The form of scientific publishing has changed substantially since the preparation of the second edition in the early 1990s with the rapid development of electronic digital means for storage and transmission of information. The ICSU Press Committee has monitored these changes from the outset and this third edition is offered as part of the process of informing the scientific community and offering advice. The guidelines do not pretend to be either normative or exhaustive and do not necessarily reflect the views of ICSU in detail, though it is intended that they should be in accord with ICSU policy statements.

Comments and suggestions are welcomed and should be sent to Dr. Dennis Shaw at Keble College, University of Oxford, OX1 3PG, United Kingdom.(e-mail: dennis.shaw@keb.ox.ac.uk). These comments will be considered by the ICSU Committee on the Dissemination of Scientific Information and the online version of the guidelines will be updated annually.

Availability of Guidelines

The guidelines are available in hard-copy from the ICSU Secretariat at 51 Boulevard de Montmorency, 75016 Paris, France. There is a small charge (US$10.00) to cover the cost of postage and packing. They are also freely available online on the ICSU Press website [associnst.ox.ac.uk/~icsuinfo/]. It is intended that the online version will be kept up to date in order to reflect the rapid changes in publishing practices and new publications, particularly online ones, as they are produced.

ICSU

In 1998 the name was changed from International Council of Scientific Unions to International Council for Science. The abbreviation (ICSU) and the aim of the organisation remains the same. ICSU has existed since 1931 to represent science at an international level, to address matters of common concern to scientists world-wide, and to create interdisciplinary bodies and programmes that cut across the compartmentalisation of science. The website [www.icsu.org] provides full information and contact names and addresses of secretariat, committee members and member organisations. Other useful sites with relevant links are those of the Society for Scholarly Publishing (USA) at www.sspnet.org/ and the Association of Learned and Professional Society Publishers (UK) at www.alpsp.org.uk/.

ICSU Press

ICSU Press is the imprint of ICSU's Committee on Dissemination of Scientific Information. It is charged with providing advice to the ICSU family on scientific publications, new developments in information technology, access to data and information, and pertinent legal issues. Further information about its activities is available from the website already cited. These Guidelines are part of its advisory function.

INASP

The terms of reference of ICSU Press also require it to pay special attention to the needs of scientists in developing countries. The International Network for the Availability of Scientific Publications is an initiative supported by ICSU. Further information about INASP and similar initiatives and the availability of scientific publications world-wide is given in chapter 10.

10

CHAPTER 1
INTRODUCTION

The Guidelines are intended for the ICSU "family" first and foremost, though it is hoped that others concerned with the communication of science will find them useful. This statement is expanded in the following section and the structure of the document explained.

1.1 The purpose of an audience for the Guidelines

The Guidelines aim to give outline guidance to learned societies that wish to publish, either acting as their own publisher or working with a publishing partner. The assumption throughout is that the learned society, which might gain useful advice from an offering like this, is relatively small and unable to support many staff with expertise in the various publishing functions. Almost everything in the document is just as relevant to a university press or other non-profit making body as to a learned society and the term "learned society" includes these other organisations. It is recognised that individual scientists using the Internet will also access these Guidelines, and, with them in mind, Appendix 1 gives brief advice.

1.2 The coverage of the Guidelines

It is emphasised that the advice is selective and not comprehensive. It is also recognised throughout that practices differ from discipline to discipline and country to country and, where there is an uncertainty about conventions or practices to follow, it is recommended that the relevant international union is approached for guidance. Their addresses and links to their websites are available on the ICSU website already mentioned in the preface and in the annual *ICSU Year Book* (available online at www.icsu.org). Reference is frequently made to sources on the Internet, which should reflect changing circumstances, in preference to sources in print. Lots of books are available in most languages on aspects of book publishing. As far as learned journals are concerned, one book stands out and is worth mentioning specifically.

It is *Journal publishing* by Gillian Page, Robert Campbell and Jack Meadows, Cambridge University Press (1997).

1.3 An explanation of the layout of the Guidelines

The Guidelines are intended for those societies that wish to act as their own publisher and for those preferring to work with a publishing partner. Most of the content is concerned with those that take the former route (chapters 5-8) while the following chapter (9) deals specifically with the relationship with the partner. The introductory chapters dealing with the development of a publishing programme (2), the choice of the medium in which the content is expressed and delivered (3), and the rights that need to be secured (4) also emphasise working without a partner. They are however equally relevant as a check-list to use in working with a partner.

The Internet has become of major and growing importance for communication in science since the last edition was written. There is extensive coverage of what making content available online means to the publisher in chapter 3, throughout the rest of the Guidelines online availability is always taken into account. In addition throughout the Guidelines and in each chapter the different practices of book and journal publishing are separately dealt with where there is a divergence in procedures and custom. These differences are sometimes important and, to a large extent, are carried over into the electronic arena. Finally chapter 10, before the first appendix intended specifically for individual scientists, touches on the flow of scientific findings around the world, whether it is the work in the developed countries reaching the developing world or scientists in developing countries making their findings known to colleagues in more developed economies. There are three other appendices intended to provide a practical fleshing out of some of the narrative of the sections.

CHAPTER 2
WHY PUBLISH?

This question is really two questions: why act as a publisher and why go to a publisher. The following section is primarily concerned with why a learned society might appropriately act as a publisher both in general and in specific terms. It is relevant for societies working with a partner as well as publishing on their own. But insofar as criteria for evaluating specific publishing proposals are considered, the section is particularly relevant in the latter case because the prospective partner to any agreement will wish to establish how publishing decisions are to be made or be directly involved in making them. Secondly this chapter touches on the question of why an individual scientist might go to a publisher, which is also briefly dealt with in Appendix 1. In addition there is some consideration of the role of the publisher and why a learned society may be well equipped to act in this role.

2.1   Communicating science.

2.1.1   The special responsibility of learned societies

Putting on one side the "business" questions that are considered in chapter 5, the answer to the question "why publish?" is that the object of the learned society publisher is "to communicate science". It could be argued that it is an intrinsic part of the role of the learned society to communicate: indeed many societies have such a role enshrined in their constitution and often a long history of publishing. The implication is that a learned society as a publisher is likely to be intrinsically committed to the role, whereas the commercial publisher receives capital or generates revenue which might be employed in another area of business altogether, where better opportunities for profit are perceived by the owners.

2.1.2   The languages of science

Communication may involve communicating research or using knowledge to instruct, it may be for local or international consumption, and it obviously need not be in the English language, although, throughout these Guidelines, English is assumed as the language of science. Nevertheless there will be some references to relevant publications in other languages, specially Spanish, at appropriate points in the text: it is hoped to build these up. The extent to which there is a flourishing local scientific literature in other languages varies from discipline to discipline. Where it does exist and particularly where there is a large population working in a major world language such as Russian or Chinese, there are usually well established translation services which enable communication both ways – from English or into English. In such circumstances learned societies, sometimes in collaboration with publishing partners, often organise translations. Such translation work needs to be considered in the same way as other publishing opportunities.

2.2   What does a publisher add?

The publisher adds value. Editing, production, marketing and distribution are brought together by the publisher. The overall control is important, though it does not matter in this context whether or not some of the functions are farmed out. The publisher provides in its name a guarantee of quality, which the reader may recognise. In the case of journals it is the title of the journal itself that is recognised by the reader. The journal is an "envelope" for the individual articles.

2.2.1   Editing

The editorial function is central. The term "editor" is difficult to translate from English. It can imply the "academic" editor who organises peer review and who makes acceptance decisions; an in-house person responsible for commissioning and organising the publishing programme; or someone internal who deals with the production process (production editor) or who is responsible for copy-editing the "manuscripts" whether typescript or electronic (sub-editor or copy-editor). To complicate matters further, an additional and important "editorial" role involves substantive changes to the text. This can be either by "polishing" the language for the scientist not working in his or her own first language or by "developing" the text to make it clearer or appropriate for the purpose – particularly important in textbook publishing. Many learned society publishers merge some of these functions and indeed some of the special strength of learned

14

society publishing is that they employ academic specialists on their staff who either act as "academic" editors or back up the "academic" editors from a position of serious knowledge of the subject. Copy-editing, which may be part of the role of such staff, is considered at greater length below as part of the production process because it too needs further definition.

2.2.2   The importance of peer review

Peer review is central to the editorial function. The quality of what is published depends on the judgement of the "invisible college" to which the author belongs being brought to bear on what he or she has written. The work of the "referee" or "reviewer" (both terms are used in the Guidelines) is usually unpaid but it is an essential part of scientific communication. The publisher may not be directly involved but it is an important part of the publisher's task to make sure that peer review is done properly and, if necessary, financially supported. The publisher may be asked to support the review process with software (to keep track of the processing of the submissions) or by providing website facilities (ftp boxes) if the editorial group wish to make full use of e-mail to speed up refereeing.

2.2.3   The organisation of peer review

The learned society publisher is particularly well placed to harness national and international scholarship for this task. There are a number of ways of organising peer review. Traditionally a book or a journal article is refereed by a number of scholars in the same field as the author. Their judgements are transmitted to the in-house editor or series editor (for books) or the (usually external) journal editor for journals and then passed on to the author anonymously. The outcome may be a recommendation to accept, to accept after revision or to reject. It is important to emphasise that referees should recommend and not decide. The experience of journal publishers is that it is best to have one editor or a group of editors who decide what to accept or reject and who are able to discern potentially important results (or discount boring ones) in the large number of submissions that require revision. For learned societies the choice of such editors can make a big difference to the success of a journal. The same principle is relevant to the way in which a book series is organised.

15

2.2.4 "Open" peer review.

It is usual for the comments of the referees to be passed on to the author without revealing the identity of the source. If there are strong criticisms, authors may be annoyed and press to know the source. Modifications of, or variations to, the process include the choice (or at least recommendation) of the names of appropriate reviewers by the author, "blind refereeing" where the name of the author is concealed from the reviewers with a view to eliminating bias or completely open reviewing. Open reviewing involves making available the names of referees to the author, and, if wished, direct contact between author and referee. Open reviewing has been extended into the online environment and submitted material is in some cases placed on open websites so that anyone accessing the site can comment or criticise. The idea is that this process will lead to the maximum scrutiny and the best end result. There has been little enthusiasm in most disciplines for open reviewing online, except among some physics communities.

2.2.5 "Sifting"

The sifting process sorts out those articles and books that are regarded as worth publishing from those that are not. It leads to a validation, a stamp of approval indicated by an acceptance, from the publisher, which is crucial to making scientific progress possible. Scientists cannot read everything written in their subject area and they need to be able to rely on the judgements of others as represented in the policies of particular publications or series. The possibility of relying on such judgements is even more important now that so much more information is available online. It is just one but the most important of the organisational functions of publishers discussed below.

2.2.6 Decision-making

Publishers must also make decisions based on the likelihood of the book or journal selling enough copies to be financially viable (see chapter 5 on publishing finance). It would be good if there were a direct link between quality, as ascertained by refereeing procedures and sales – but there is not. It is difficult to sell many copies of a book or gain many subscribers to a journal if the quality is not high enough, but the converse is not true: not all good books or journals sell. Learned society publishers have to take marketing seriously and marketing involves understanding the market and its demands as well as trying to reach it. Unfortunately there is usually no way in which the publisher can make a serious judgement about the likely sale of a book or journal except by being guided by experience of previous similar publications. It is not always easy to find a publication sufficiently similar on a small list for any conclusions to be reached. Nevertheless learned societies do have the advantage of their membership and often highly experienced officers who have a lot of experience of what their peers want. Focus groups and proactive investigation of what the market wants is usually an expense too far but judicious sounding out of the relevant part of the membership can give pointers to likely interest in the marketplace.

2.3   How can a publisher best serve science?

The learned society in its role as a publisher can best serve science by doing what it can do best. Its strength lies in the fact that it represents a discipline. In most cases, it would be difficult to argue that learned societies are best equipped to reach the general public. So-called "trade" publishing of books is difficult to undertake successfully without employing or making use of highly trained promotion staff familiar with advanced marketing techniques and a team of representatives who call on booksellers. Magazines are equally expensive to handle. These Guidelines therefore will not deal with the special practices of trade or consumer publishing as it is called. Learned society publishers, because of the authority they can bring to the task, have a special advantage in publishing science. The publication of a properly refereed and produced national journal can foster local scholarship. Sometimes the proceedings of a symposium covering important but specialised research devoted to, for example, a specific disease of local importance will not be made available except through a learned society's sponsorship and financial support.

CHAPTER 3
THE CHALLENGE OF ELECTRONIC PUBLISHING

The need to decide on a medium of communication, whether the publication should be in print or electronic form or both, is a new requirement. The role of publishers must be to make available and deliver what they publish in whatever way best enables the intended audience to access or receive it. It is with this principle in mind that the decision should be made.

This chapter is concerned with the decision whether to publish electronically, either in that form only or in combination with a print publication. The emphasis is on journals.

3.1   The Internet

3.1.1   The Internet as the state of the art
Since the last edition of the Guidelines was produced the development of the Internet, particularly with the emergence of the World Wide Web, has been the single biggest change impacting on publishing practice and potential and may indeed be the biggest change since the invention of printing. Print is no longer the sole medium for scholarly publishing. In 1994, when the last edition was prepared, electronic publishing was confined almost entirely to putting data on a CD ROM or perhaps including a disc in the back of a book. Presentations of data in this form are still useful but CD ROM as a way of publishing primary content has now mainly been rejected. Electronic publishing now usually means going on to the World Wide Web as a serious alternative or addition to print publishing.

3.1.2   Journals online
The Internet is much more important for journals publishing than it is in the case of books. In what follows, there are distinctions to be made between electronic only journals where there is no print version, print journals which are made available in an identical electronic form, and

journals which have print and electronic versions that differ. There has been some attempt to adopt terminology to distinguish between these three different types of publication but, as this is not generally recognised as yet, it is not used in these Guidelines. Although at the start of 1999 it was estimated that only a small percentage of all the scholarly journals available for sale had online versions or were totally electronic the majority of the major titles now have electronic versions. The trend is for these versions to begin to diverge from the print versions. Electronic only journals are slower to take off than had been anticipated by some. For an optimistic approach it is worth looking at the writings of Peter Boyce on the website of the American Astronomical Society (www.aas.org). This society publishes electronic journals that are the normative versions in that the enhanced online content represents the definitive publication while an optional print version is regarded as a cut down selection of the complete message. It is part of a farsighted policy resulting from a lot of thought over a period of time and which appears to have received the approval of the membership (or authors). There are special characteristics of the astronomical community that do help but the overall achievement is impressive: is this relevant to all disciplines? Societies in some developing countries have found the online medium one to be preferred in order that the international audience can be reached. INASP has been particularly active in facilitating this development. Particular mention should be made of *Electronic Journal Publishing: A Reader* (see oneworld.org/inasp/psi/ejp/preface.html). In an introductory essay Sally Morris has provided both an excellent guide to the pros and cons of electronic journal publishing and a check-list of decisions. It is often argued that the electronic only journal is cheaper to produce, and that online versions can reach more readers and more quickly. There is truth in all these assertions but a downside too, which will be examined below. In addition to these advantages there also needs to be taken into account the extra functionality provided by the Internet that may enable a more sophisticated, comprehensive or useful message to be delivered from scientist to scientist.

3.1.3   Archiving

One of the biggest deterrents to scientific authors submitting to electronic only journals is concern about archiving. Print publications have been traditionally archived by national libraries and in many countries policies are being developed to archive the national electronic heritage also. Some learned societies have pledged themselves to maintain an archive of their own publications prepared in an electronic medium. Nevertheless these initiatives are not yet fully developed and are in some countries not practicable. For further discussion see www.icsti.org, the website of the International Council for Scientific and Technical Information which is a scientific associate of ICSU.

3.2 Costs

There are a lot of data about costs in the electronic arena summarised usefully in the ICSU Press workshop held in Oxford in spring 1998 and available on the ICSU Press website. The general view is that it is significantly more expensive to publish journals in both print and online versions than it is to publish in either medium alone but cheaper to publish online only than print only. The difference however is smaller than some claim. Most of the costs of running a journal are incurred before a single copy is printed and the difference in costs, electronic only compared with print only, lies in savings on printing and distribution. A more significant qualification relates to the cost of maintaining the infrastructure. The costs of maintaining a server, including the costs of the technical staff who maintain and exploit its potential, have to be factored in to any cost calculation. In addition, if the journal is sold rather than made available free of charge, access has to be controlled so that only those who have paid can download the content: management systems to control access are not cheap to install and maintain

3.3 Editorial consequences

The emphasis here is on some of the editorial changes, which electronic publishing of journals and also of books (see section 3.3.4) bring about and which are not dealt with elsewhere in these guidelines. The aim is to present problems (which are easily overlooked) but not to discourage initiatives. Rights are discussed in chapter 4.

3.3.1 Possibilities of the electronic format.

The content of a journal can be the same as the content of the "same" journal online, which means that there is no need to change peer review processes (for example) – though these can be expedited. An online version however can also carry extra illustrations; colour which is too expensive to print; and dynamic illustrations such as rotating structures. In particular hypertext links are possible from references in the text, and in some systems at the end of an article, to an abstract of that article in a secondary database and through this gateway, to the full text of the article. The linking can be either within the same journal or within the journals or books published by the same publisher or, given agreements, across a range of journals. It can be argued that "linking" is the single most important contribution made to scientific communication by the adoption of online publishing.

3.3.2 Impact on the refereeing process

The opportunities presented by the exploitation of Internet functionality generate new problems that are not just a matter of increased costs. There is the difference additional types of content make to the refereeing process. If a "dynamic" item, an electronic object, is part of the message of the article it has to be treated as such and refereed as such: publishers are only now learning how to handle this. At least one major learned society publisher will not accept the submission of an article which contains links to unrefereed additional material held on the website of the author. If it is part of the article additional content has also to be preserved and archived (see section 3.1.3 above). Mention has been made of the claim that journal articles can be made available quicker online than they can in print. It has to be pointed out that the big delay for most journals is between submission and acceptance and not between acceptance and publication. Use of email to communicate between referees and the editorial group, and a policy of demanding electronic files from authors to be lodged on an ftp site accessible only to referees, can speed up the refereeing process to some extent. It cannot however create extra time in the busy lives of those doing the work. Publishers always have to fight to get their referees to prioritise the work they are asked to do on a journal. It can also lead to problems if articles are put online on acceptance. Usually they cannot have page numbers and thus cannot be cited. In addition they may be withdrawn before they are made available in print. Many publishers that have online versions of print journals make articles available only when the issue concerned has gone to press

21

3.3.3 The outreach of electronic journals

Nevertheless there is a great deal of excitement in the outreach of electronic journals especially if the economics of the publisher allows them to be made available free to anyone in the world who is interested. In print secondary publishers do not reference journals published by learned societies in many developing countries, even though they are rigorously reviewed and produced to a high standard, and articles tend to be incorrectly cited even when noticed. It is incorrectly considered that the Internet enables more notice to be taken of a publication. If the attention of the community served by a journal is drawn to its online existence (such as by means mentioned in section 3.6) it can certainly be accessed more easily than in the print environment if such access if free. Even where the journal is priced it can mean that a journal, once only available in a library in print form, can in an online version now be brought to the desktop of every interested researcher served by that library. The downside is currently the lack of prestige. The electronic medium is associated with unregulated information and fully refereed journals find it difficult at present to attract authors. The difficulties already mentioned of archiving electronic only journals (or divergent electronic versions), is put forward as a main reason for this distrust in the scientific community but it may be more a matter of conservatism.

3.3.4 Putting books online

Publishers can be badly misled by the concepts of "multiple media" or "media neutral" which are much bandied about. What publishing in more than one medium means for books needs to be looked at closely or foolish decisions may be made. Very little book material has so far been put online. It is straightforward to put text online without alteration but who wants to download a whole book? There is every evidence that scientists do not want to read as distinct from search and scan on screen. There have been attempts to provide textbook chapters that can be picked and mixed to make a new customised book in both the print and electronic environments. This has not worked very well partly because material to be used in this way has to be written using a different approach (for example by making each chapter self-contained and not referring to other chapters) for the resulting book to work as an entity. Some individual chapters are also being made available like journal articles: some of objections already mentioned apply here too. To provide instructional material in an electronic format so that it is read online involves using the opportunities presented in the Internet environment for different "threads" that allow an argument to be developed in a non-linear form. This demands a lot of editorial guidance to the author who has to visualise a progression of different frames. The easiest book content to make available electronically in addition to a print format is reference or encyclopaedic material where online entries are discrete items which can nevertheless make use of the functionality of the Internet already mentioned in the discussion of journals.

3.4   Deciding arrangements for hosting

The term "hosting" refers to the making available on a website whatever content whether just promotional or including actual publications the publisher wishes to put online: a publisher can do the job alone or work with another.

3.4.1   Management issues

It is quite cheap to set up a website and the cost of memory comes down all the time and is already at a stage when it is not a barrier to putting up lots of material. The main problem lies in trying to manage the server, to make it possible to locate and draw out what is needed, to enable navigation from searcher to content, but above all to manage access which is crucial if the publications concerned are seen as a source of revenue. Unless access can be managed, so that only those who have paid can access and download that journal or book, article or chapter, which they have paid for, income cannot be earned from online publications. This statement is true both for journals and for books. Management systems are expensive and a number of quite large publishers have suffered financially from commitments to particular systems that have turned out not to deliver what was promised. The fact that library preferences are changing, as far as making available journals for their communities is concerned, complicates decisions relating to access management. A year or so ago libraries were willing, if reluctant, to administer passwords. Now they prefer that the publisher's management system recognise a range of IP addresses (the identifying number for an individual machine) with passwords only used in order to give access to users offsite or on vacation. Most recently librarians are beginning to find IP addresses irksome to work with and new systems are being developed which the publisher has to become aware of. Publishers cannot afford to ignore the ways in which their audience uses available technology if they wish to bring their publications to the biggest audience.

3.4.2 Specialist help

It may be possible to get help or indeed support from the computer service of a local university. There are some particularly helpful sources of information available online from the help desks of some major universities. It is however usually best to go to a specialist company or organisation, of which there are a growing number, if online publishing is seen as both a serious proposition and a source of income. Some of these specialists offer help, some offer hosting arrangements for a cost and some can provide managed access to content hosted on the site of the publisher. INASP in particular, and ICSU Press may be able to put enquirers in the right direction.

3.5 Production implications

3.5.1 Asking for discs

In many disciplines it is possible to ask authors to provide their articles on a disc which has been formatted in accordance with the style of the journal. This is particularly true in mathematics and the physical sciences where TeX is the standard software used. Mention of the instructions for authors, which need to be prepared, is made in chapter 7.1. The advantages of working with electronic files in the refereeing process has already been touched on (see section 3.3.1). However many scientists cannot deliver their manuscripts electronically and in some disciplines the multiplicity of different types of software used creates serious problems for the publisher that cannot ask reasonably for one format.

3.5.2 Formats available

This sub-section approaches the question of format from the point of view of the user rather than the author. Much online journal content is now made available in either or both PDF (portable document format) and files tagged using SGML (Standard General Mark-Up Language). PDF enables all the richness of the print page to be presented on screen.

SGML, converted into its web derivative HTML, enables the linking (for example from references to abstracts or even full text of the articles referred to) which is perhaps the most important part of the added functionality of the Internet. It is not as straightforward as this. Versions of PDF, now widely available, enable linking outside the document and a full structured version is planned. Even more currently exciting is the emergence of XML (Extensible Mark-up Language) which makes it possible to link a particular text item to a number of different sources on the Internet. The situation as it is now can be summarised as follows. Many major publishers provide their journals in both PDF and SGML (HTML) formats. Often, the full-text of the journal article is available in PDF, but the header information (the title, author, affiliation, abstract and keywords) is tagged in HTML. There is a particular useful article by Bill Kasdorf (SGML and PDF – Why We Need Both) in *The Journal of Electronic Publishing* (see www.press.umich.edu/jep/03-04/kasdorf.html).

3.5.3   The creation of the formats

Both these formats can be created in-house; appropriate software for the task is available. There are a number of decisions which need to be taken into account when the work is done by the publisher, particularly where a supplier has to be instructed. PDF can be produced in-house using PDF Writer but a better result can in practice be gained if it is "distilled" by a supplier from PostScript, the *de facto* standard Page Description Language that numerous typesetting systems can produce as an end product. Instructions have to be given because of the numerous optional settings, especially regarding figure resolutions and security, which need to be specified. As for SGML, an appropriate DTD (document type definition) has to be settled on. This requires serious structural analysis of the material that is being coded, plus complicated processing to convert a structural format to a display format, as well as strict integrity-checking procedures (parsing) There are lots of DTDs available some of which suit one purpose (or intermediary) and some another. Fortunately there is some degree of convergence.

3.5.4   The importance of the customer

The production manager has to have a very clear and exact idea of what the electronic file is needed for and who it is to be used by. At the start of the production process authors have to be told how they should present their articles and preferably templates have to be prepared for them. Customers, particularly libraries and those intermediaries that provide online interfaces, have their needs or even demands, which must be taken into account in deciding on the format of the electronic file. The manager also has to be able to communicate this to the supplier, the typesetter or compositor, and to make sure that the specifications are understood. Even the largest publishers have had difficulties in producing electronic files to a consistent standard.

3.5.5 Costs

There is also a cost involved especially if both formats are being adopted. It is necessary at the moment to handle PDF and SGML separately. Two different operations are involved – both incurring costs. The overall charge will be at least twenty per cent additional over standard typesetting charges if one is using an external supplier. The real costs of doing the work in-house will not necessarily be lower

3.6　Marketing possibilities

3.6.1　Saving money

It is possible to save money using the Internet to reach the desired audience as an alternative to traditional methods of promotion. At the same time there is growing evidence that using the Internet for marketing is effective in terms of sales.

3.6.2　Using listservs and email

Characteristically, promotion involves sending out lots of bits of paper. Transmission of the same information over the Internet can be virtually free and also much more targeted. Each sub-discipline has its "listservs" and it is usually acceptable for a learned society to post information about books and journals on them, for example tables of contents and also ordering information. If not the publisher should turn to journal editors and editorial boards and book authors, editors or contributors for help in putting up this information and indeed for providing lists of email addresses. The readers of such listservs or bulletin boards are a key audience for books and journals.

3.6.3 "Passive" promotion

Certainly information about publications can be created in HTML format and just placed on a website. It is always there and always accessible. There are few constraints of space. It can be updated whenever there is time – though it is important that staff time is allocated for the updating.

3.6.4 Making the website visible.

Try to include important relevant words in your HTML "title", your URL, and the first few lines of text on each page. Encourage lots of people to link to you. This will have benefits in itself but will also enhance your ranking in some search engines. Other learned societies and similar organisations may well be willing to put an icon on their website which points to this information source in return for reciprocal arrangements. If you submit your website to Infoseek, Altavista, Excite, HotBot and Lycos you have covered the really important search engines. For more information see http://searchenginewatch.com/webmasters/index.html. If you wish to use frames or JavaScript on your site, to improve its appearance and enhance navigation, remember that search engine spiders (webcrawlers) cannot get at your text so do provide a non-frames version for them and for many of your users as well. In addition there are all sorts of clever ways of making sure that people throughout the world that might be interested in a site reach it through search engines, for example by the use of "keyword" and "description" metatags. For information about the creation of metatags see the following website: vancouver-webpages.com/META/mk-metas.html.

3.6.5 Sample copies

Sample issues of journals and chapters of books can also be made accessible on a website, making the costly business of mailing sample material free, except for the cost of putting the material up, and it is much easier both for the publisher to administer and for the potential customer to acquire. Alternatively forms, for obtaining print samples can be posted and easily accessed.

3.7   Standards

3.7.1   International information available online

As is the case in the print medium (see chapter 5) the adoption of the most appropriate standards in the electronic arena makes a publication more accessible. It also saves money for the publisher both directly and also indirectly because the costs to other parts of the information chain are lowered. Standards are beginning to emerge but are not universally used or indeed available. The central source of standard information is the website of the International Standards Organisation (ISO) in Geneva at www.iso.ch. ISO recommend that enquirers should first contact their local members, that offer information and customer services with regard not only to international standards and standardising activities, but also to national and regional standards, regulations, certification and related activities that do not fall directly within their remit. They provide a list of local members. ISO makes provision for a number of language groups but some have found the site difficult to navigate. Particularly useful is a forthcoming *Reader on Standards*, which is being provided by INASP (see chapter 10). This will provide a number of useful references.

3.7.2   Local information available online

The UK Book Industry Communication site www.bic.org.uk is a particularly useful guide to international standards connected with electronic publishing and in particular electronic data interchange, the interface where the interests of the publisher and bookshops/ agents/vendors world-wide should coincide. In spite of the name of the organisation, the standards described apply to both books and journals. More heavyweight information is available at a US site, that of the National Information Standards Organization (NISO) on www.niso.org. This site does have information in a number of languages. Another useful site, British again but a guidance to the range of standards which need to be considered, is the eLib Standards Guidelines at www.ukoln.ac.uk/services/elib/papers/other/standards which recommends the selection and use of standards for the British higher education sector's electronic library programme.

3.7.3   The Digital Object Identifier

In section 6.4 the importance of using international standard book and serial numbers is mentioned. The equivalent in the electronic arena will probably be the digital object identifier (DOI), although it is not just an identifier but also a persistent locator. The publishing community set up the Foundation responsible for the DOI because the main aim behind the creation of the DOI is to enable content-holders to trade electronically. Like the ISBN and the ISSN the reason for the creation of this system is to enable publications to be bought and sold. It is now supported by all parts of the information chain and the whole system is under active development. The DOI is applicable to any digital object which can be a journal article or a book chapter or an object (an illustration for example) within either. It is not too early for publishers to consider opting into the system which is described in detail at www.doi.org. However because there are costs involved many smaller publishers will wish only to take the first step which is to make sure that all the components of all their publications that may be sold are clearly and consistently identified, even if only for internal purposes. It is not a matter of selling a product. In the electronic arena in particular the sale of rights is central. There are some clear and cogent position papers on the DOI site, which is very regularly updated.

3.7.4 Metadata

The term "Metadata" is usually defined as "data about data". It is not a new concept but rather a new term that encompasses familiar types of information like bibliographical records, identifiers and many computer databases. Because all electronic commodities can be described as "data", all data about electronic commodities are "metadata". It has been realised that for the DOI to work standardisation of metadata is essential. Metadata as a term is too recent to be accepted by many spell checkers and so the section on common questions at www.indecs.org may be essential to many.

CHAPTER 4
ACQUIRING RIGHTS

This chapter is written from the point of view of the learned society publisher. The section on contracts sets out the sort of clauses that need to be covered in different types of contracts with editors, authors or contributors. Other sections discuss what rights need to be acquired, the use of the rights granted, permissions, licences, "foreign" rights and finally contractual procedures adopted within the publishing company. One definition can usefully be given here. Rights acquired by the publisher are upstream rights. Rights granted by the publisher are downstream rights. In Appendix 1 to the Guidelines there are recommendations to the scientific author concerning the same issues which are more or less the same. There should be no need for any divergence between the positions adopted; if there are the learned society will have to consider whether they are properly representing the interests of their community. Contracts between a learned society and a publishing partner are considered in chapter 9.

4.1   Contracts

This section concentrates on the principles behind contractual arrangements and gives specifics where models are not easily available in handbooks.

4.1.1   The formalising of a relationship

A publisher adds value to material created by another – the author. In scholarly publishing the author is not usually an employee of the publisher and in what follows this normal situation is assumed. In any case, it is crucial that the relationship between publisher and author is formalised by a contract, however short. This is not a matter of bureaucracy: a contract prevents misunderstandings. Characteristically, learned societies have difficulties with the concept of contracts. If the editor of a journal owned by a learned society is a prominent member of Council, why bother with a legal document? Such societies, if there is a change of policy or the person concerned is not capable of doing the job properly, find real problems if there is no formal arrangement with the individual.

4.1.2 Changing circumstances

In past years publishers, including commercial publishers, have treated contracts casually. Copyright lines have been put on books or journals where no copyright has been transferred and copyright transfer agreements have not been preserved reliably. Contributors to symposium proceedings or multi-authored books have not been given any form of contract. Now there is a much greater sensitivity to intellectual property issues in part due to the changed circumstances of electronic publishing. It is for example becoming common to transform what used to be a matter of custom (the relationship between journal publishers and subscription agents) to an arrangement governed by a quite complex agreement (the relationship between online journal publishers and subscription agents and others as online intermediaries). Such contracts assume that the publisher has acquired all rights necessary from the authors of all the articles in their journals for the intermediaries to do their job. A few authors have begun to seek further reward when content provided by them for print publication is now made available online and a larger number of authors desire some sort of control over what is done with their work. The importance of some sort of contract to cover all content in all publications cannot be overemphasised. Likewise contracts have to be lodged carefully (see section 4.7).

4.1.3 Contract with book authors

The most authoritative book on book contracts is *Publishing Agreements – A Book of Precedents* edited by Clark, Owen and Palmer: Butterworth, London (5th edition 1997). Though based on English law it aims to be useful throughout the world. Unfortunately even in its latest edition it does not cover all types of contract that even a small publisher may have to come to terms with and it concentrates heavily on book publishing.

4.1.4 General principles relating to all contracts

In what follows questions that should be taken into account in framing contracts with journal editors are covered in more detail. Throughout the world, new laws are being enacted – often reflecting international treaties – to take into account the changing circumstances, particularly regarding rights transferred, brought about by the emergence of the Internet. With this in mind and also because legal environments are not the same throughout the world, publishers should always take advice from lawyers locally, taking care to choose a lawyer who specialises in publishing contracts. A learned society publisher needs to prepare contracts for book authors and editors, contributors to books, journal editors and authors of articles in journals. Guidelines such as these can only outline what needs to be in what type of contract and, in any case, the strictly "legal" parts of such contracts vary according to the jurisdiction. This is especially true of the head or main contract with an author or an editor, for example, rather than that with a contributor. The following general points are worth attending to. Practices in scholarly publishing often differ from those in "consumer" publishing, and clauses appropriate to book publishing are not always the same as those for journals publishing. It is important that all contracts are comprehensible, or at least explicable, to both parties. It is also important that they reflect operational realities, the way in which the parties are likely to work together. Finally the publishing arm of a learned society must always remain aware that it has a duty to protect the society should legal action be brought as a result of an infringement of publishing law. Contracts have to be worded so as to prevent or minimise an adverse judgement: clauses incorporating such safeguards for the publisher often appear draconian to the author and cannot always be maintained.

4.1.5 Elements common to head contracts

There are certain elements that are common to most head contracts.. Book contracts must allow for what happens if the author does not deliver on time and, later on in the process, if a new edition is required. Contracts with a journal editor must make clear when the relationship terminates in normal circumstances and what is to be done to terminate a relationship if something goes wrong. Learned society publishers have to take a tough view and, in the past, they have not done so: they cannot afford for a major source of their income to be run down because of personal deficiencies of one of their members. Contracts are to some extent instructional. They represent an agreement between publisher and author about their respective roles in the publishing process and about the nature of the publication, what it is, how many pages, and when it is to be handed in. They are also concerned with the financial relationship if there is one. If royalties are given it is imperative that the contract makes clear what the percentage due to the author is based on. If it is the "list price" it must be made clear in what country. If it is on "net receipts", the definition of this problematical term must be part of the contract. There is a case for using terms such as income or revenue "received by the publisher" but even in those circumstances there must be no doubt about who the publisher is – not always clear if the learned society is selling at a discount to a distributor or co-publisher. It is also important to be clear about the accounting period, the period during which the sales are made on which the royalties are calculated, and also the date on which the royalties are paid. There is ample scope for friction between publisher and author/editors if this is not spelt out and in time acted on.

4.1.6   A contract with a journal editor

Because journal publishing is so important to learned societies and because it is difficult to find an up-to-date contract with a journal editor in current reference sources, a sample contract has been included as Appendix 2 to these Guidelines. The contract is written in the context of the Law of England and Wales and assumes a journal that is in print with an electronic equivalent. It allows for the special needs of medical publishing and brackets indicate some sections relevant only to medical publishing. It should be used with caution. Other jurisdictions have different laws and laws change. Some of the clauses can be removed without problems and others are crucial. It is always best to go to a lawyer with relevant experience.

4.2   What rights are actually needed?

The transfer or licensing of rights from the author to the publisher is central in all publishing contracts. In this section some general principles are discussed. Because the transfer or licensing of rights by authors of journal articles to publishers is such an important and sensitive matter, Appendix 3 at the end of the Guidelines provides some sample wordings.

4.2.1   Rights and warranties

Legislation relating to intellectual property rights varies from country to country: in some jurisdictions some of the rights of the author, known as moral rights, are inherent and cannot be transferred. Moral rights in UK law are explained in the book by Clark and others (see section 4.1.3). For the publisher, the basic need is for the author to transfer those rights that will enable the publisher to do its job and that these rights are granted explicitly and in writing. In addition authors should always be asked to warrant that they own or are licensed to use all relevant rights in what they wish to have published, that the material submitted contains no unlawful statements and does not infringe the rights of others, and (depending on publishing policies) that the material has not been published before. The publisher should provide authors with standard forms which they are urged to use in seeking permission to quote, or use illustrations from another publication (see section 4.6 and Appendix 4).

4.2.2   Copyright or publishing rights?

It has been customary for a publisher to ask for a transfer of copyright from their authors. Most publishers find this the best way to make sure that they have the rights they need. In the USA for example most learned society publishers consider that they cannot be certain of their position unless they are assigned copyright. On the other hand some publishers now ask only to be granted an exclusive right to publish. This is common in book publishing world-wide. In some jurisdictions, particularly those not related to US or UK law, publishers feel able only (or may only be entitled) to ask for the transference of specific rights, which should include print, reprographic, digitisation, electronic publishing and permissions rights. They may need to itemise exactly what they want from the author, which demands some care.

4.2.3   Exceptions to and insistence on contractual arrangements with journal authors

It is good practice for publishers to make sure that they insist on the author agreeing to whatever clauses covering transfer of rights have been decided on. There have to be exceptions in the case of some companies that own the copyrights of employees or where the author is a US government employee or of some other governments, where copyright is in the public domain and thus cannot be granted. If, however, there are lots of different arrangements the publisher will find it hard to keep account of what rights are transferred which makes it difficult to be secure about entering into downstream contracts or licences with such as intermediaries (see section 4.4 on licensing). In all cases it is reasonable for an author to expect that specific rights are explicitly retained or granted back. The reasonable demand that this is done comes particularly from journal publishing where it is not normal to give any financial reward to the author of a primary article. Books of precedents do not yet cover such arrangements so it is worth providing one sample wording in Appendix 3 at the end of the Guidelines. In the final analysis situations may come up when the author will not grant the rights requested. In such situations it is recommended that publishers decline to publish.

4.2.4 Registration of copyright

In some countries copyright should be registered: in most there are no formalities. Publishers need to take responsibility for checking what the situation is and acting on behalf of the author. It is recommended that the international copyright symbol © plus the word "copyright" followed by the name of the copyright owner and the year of publication should be printed in a prominent position. The same principle extends to the electronic environment. In a book the copyright line usually appears on the verso of the title page and in a journal at the bottom of the first page of each article. The words "All Rights Reserved" can be added or a longer wording explaining which rights are handled by reproduction rights organisations. On this question see the next section (4.3).

4.3 Making use of rights transferred to the publisher

The author is entitled to expect that the publisher will make use of any rights granted. There are a number of ways in which these rights can be used and they are listed in this section and the following two. Copyright licensing schemes provide another source of income but, more important, enable the would-be user of material owned by the publisher to get permission easily and to pay for it. A growing number of countries now have such schemes that exist to permit reproduction of journal articles and sections of books where such reproduction is not covered by statutory exceptions to copyright such as fair use or fair dealing arrangements in UK and US law. The International Federation of Reproduction Rights Organisations (IFRRO) provides a list of such organisations in different countries and administers the processes by which money from transactional fees and blanket arrangements is transferred from country to country. IFRRO is to be found at Rue de Prince Royal 87, B-1050 Brussels, Belgium. The fax number is +32 2 551 08 95 and the website is at www.copyright.com/ifrro/. Exactly how users pay varies a great deal from country to country. It can be through a tax on photocopying machines, through blanket licences or transactional licences to name three ways in use.

4.4   Licensing

4.4.1   Licensing digital information

The very term "intellectual property" applied to the activities of scientific publishers rather than say patents and their exploitation is a recent phenomenon, almost entirely due to the changed circumstances resulting from putting content, particularly journals, on the Internet. In the past content was sold. Now it is usually leased. Licences characteristically cover the making available of electronic versions of journals to libraries where networking to end-users and specifically what the end-user can do with the articles available at the desktop, is not covered by existing copyright law. Agreements with those intermediaries, that come between publishers and their audience, particularly libraries, are even more complex. The terms of these contracts cannot be covered here but for both parties it is best that clear non-legal wording language is used. There is no book which offers up to date guidance but the recommendations available on the Yale "liblicense" website (*Licensing Digital Information*) at www.library.yale.edu/~llicense/, intended for librarians, are invaluable to publishers too. A particularly useful "Model Licence" drawn up by a committee comprising both publishers and librarians is to be found at www.ukoln.ac.uk/services/elib/papers/pa/.

4.4.2   Electronic document delivery

One area of licensing that is much talked about is the making available of individual electronic documents, predominantly journal articles, for appropriate payment. This is sometimes known as "edocdel" or electronic document delivery. Predictions have been made that articles from those journals regarded as not of core interest for the community served by a library will be paid for "by the drink". So far use of the commercial services available has been disappointing. Most major

subscription agents are offering or intend to offer services that provide a return in the form of a fee to publishers. Other companies concerned with this sort of business are ingenta (www.ingenta.com) and Carl/ Uncover (www.carl.org).

4.4.3   Centralised Licensing

There is much discussion in many countries which will eventually lead to licensing schemes on a national basis coming to deal with the electronic environment but on the whole they are at present concerned with permission to digitise content only available in print – so-called "retrodigitisation". An example already announced can be found on the website of the British copyright licensing agency (www.cla.co.uk)

4.5   Foreign rights

For some book publishers the sale or purchase of translation rights is a regular part of their business, though this is less common in scientific book publishing than in trade publishing except in the case of textbooks. Translation rights have a special significance to many authors and, if the publisher acquires copyright or exclusive rights to publish, it is the duty of the publisher to sell these rights. This is a specialist area and there are often occasions when the publisher may be advised either to outsource the selling or to grant such rights back to the author. There is specialist software available to keep track of rights transactions but investment in this is not recommended unless a publisher has a lot of such business to deal with.

4.6 Permissions

Publishers need to be concerned with seeking and granting permissions. They need to insist that an author of any material that they publish must secure the agreement from the copyright holder for illustrations or quotations incorporated in the article or chapter concerned. It is important to make sure that non-exclusive rights in all media and territories are secured. Appropriate forms, which the author can be asked to use, are now often placed on the publisher's website. An example is given in Appendix 4. It is generally the practice for scholarly publishers to give such permissions free except in circumstances where a lot of money has been spent preparing an illustration such as a surgical drawing or where the party asking for permission intends to use the illustration or quotation for significant commercial gain. The situation is very different in trade publishing and publishers will find that the use of illustrations from contemporary painters, or quotations from recently written poems is prohibitively expensive. It is important to get permission to use illustrations for book or journal covers.

4.7 Contractual procedures

There are two significant types of procedure which, although they involve staff time being taken up by what may seem bureaucracy, are worth putting into practice. In the first place it is important to hold the contracts securely, preferably in a place set aside for this purpose, perhaps a safe for main contracts; and certainly not in an "editorial" or "marketing" file; otherwise contracts get lost. The importance of making sure that all content in all publications is covered by grants of rights needs to be carried through to the setting up of internal systems which log in the fact that the contract has been received. A record should also be kept of the terms of the contract if there is any variation from the norm. This is particularly important in multi-authored books and journals. Permissions to use illustrations on books or journal covers must be obtained and explicit permission is needed if these illustrations are reproduced online, even if this is only for promotional purposes.

CHAPTER 5
BASIC PUBLISHING FINANCE

There are plenty of books on basic finance. There are special problems in publishing because forecasting is very inexact. This is not due to any intrinsic inability manifested by publishing staff but because each publication is different from others previously published. In the case of electronic publishing, costs are very difficult to control because of the rapid technological change: most of these costs have been outlined in the previous section on choice of medium.

5.1   Are you aiming to make a surplus?

Many established learned society programmes run at a significant surplus and indeed support the other activities of the society. Even if these other activities are self-financing, it is important to plan for a surplus, as there is an element of uncertainty in the financial return of even the best-run publishing programme, aiming merely to cover costs is not sensible and is likely to lead to a real loss.

5.2   Making decisions

ICSU Press has for some time urged learned societies never to commit themselves to publishing programmes without setting up dedicated publishing committees. Such committees should have a responsibility to examine the potential for publication of other activities of the society, for example series of symposia, and to make a careful audit of the likely commercial consequences of what is proposed. Such committees should report back to the Council of the society in a structured way so as to restrain over-enthusiasm and to ensure that publishing policies remain in line with the overall objectives of the organisation. Plans to make a heavy investment in a book series should be evaluated with particular care as, even if all goes well, it takes time for income from sales to cover the up-front expenditure involved, and, if print-runs have been over-optimistic, a serious deficit in society finances can result. It is very difficult to estimate likely growth in journal subscriptions year-on-year and allowance must be made for a long period before revenue exceeds real costs and a longer period before cumulative losses and notional interest on these losses are covered. Only then does real profit or surplus come about. The treasurer of any society should always be closely involved in decision-making.

5.3 Cashflow and collecting money.

5.3.1 Forecasting cashflow

Financial planning for publishing is much the same as any sort of financial planning. Cashflow as a concept is mentioned here specifically because it is of central importance. Societies rarely have lots of spare income and, before any publishing programme is embarked upon, a realistic cashflow forecast should be set out as well as the more immediately accessible projected profit and loss statement. Books and journals have different cashflow profiles and this should be taken into account.

5.3.2 Cashflow from journal publishing

Journals have the merit of being paid for up-front. Most of the money should come in before any production or distribution costs are incurred because subscription agents tend to be paid by libraries before the end of the year previous to the journal volume concerned. One way to make sure that this happens is to refuse to send out any issues before payment has been received, though there are those that think that there are sound reasons for sending out one free issue before discontinuing the supply. It is a great deal of help to both publisher and subscription agent if the publisher invests in electronic data interchange (EDI) software which enables a much quicker transfer of renewal information and saves money for both parties.

5.3.3 Cashflow from book publishing

The production costs of books may have to be paid before publication or soon after and before the sales are made. Income from sales made to booksellers and agents take time to be passed on. Every effort should be made to get firm orders in before publication, through marketing or arrangements with distributors. A symposium volume may pay for its costs before publication if sales to participants in the symposium are made part of the registration fee, but the nature of such volumes is that subsequent sales are likely to be minimal and they have no backlist value (continued sales year after year).

5.3.4 Collecting money

It is vital that the collection of money due, from customers, distributors, agents and bookstores, should be given priority. It is important not only that dates for payment should be set out clearly in the terms of trade agreed but that a credit control function should be set up to make sure that these terms are enforced. Not every small publisher can afford a specialist credit control function and they may wish to consider outsourcing.

5.4 Dealing with foreign currency

Many smaller organisations find that dealing with foreign currency, in circumstances where a large proportion of sales income comes from abroad, is a particularly difficult and costly experience. Before any publishing programme is commenced, the society needs to discuss with its bank local capabilities and likely charges. It is especially important to take sound financial advice where income is received in a foreign currency, which is often the case with journals, and buying or selling currency forward should be investigated. The use of credit cards, in spite of the commission involved, enables currency problems to be circumvented for a growing number of purchases.

5.5 Staff

The financial policies of the society may involve the allocation of general overheads, such as the costs of running the building, to different functions within the society. There are also specific overhead costs such as telecommunications, and postage, which are obviously applicable. However the forecasting of how much staff time publishing takes is a particular problem. Many operations involved in publishing are labour-intensive. An obvious example is the sending off of parcels of books. Some functions, for example marketing, may involve the employment of specialised and more expensive staff. Many learned societies have made the mistake of underpaying staff who in consequence may not always have the expertise required. A realistic assessment of staff-time involved in publishing operations should be part of financial planning. There are also extra costs incurred in going online: it is very important to allow not only for the costs of employing more technical and expensive staff but also for retraining existing staff for their new roles in a rapidly changing environment.

5.6   Pricing

5.6.1   Trying out projections

The setting of the price is one of the most important decisions to be made for any publication. All the costs involved in producing, marketing, and distributing a book or a journal should be taken into account and this should be done on a cashflow basis as well as a profit and loss calculation. It is not difficult to buy or get written simple software to make life easier in trying out different financial scenarios flowing from different prices and/or print runs. The actual return in income from a distribution arrangement is mentioned in chapter 8. Royalty and similar payments should be factored in and not forgotten.

5.6.2   Pricing to market and controlling costs

There is a danger in looking at pricing from the point of view mentioned in the previous subsection, what is known as a "costs plus" viewpoint. For most publications, the market-place has expectations of a "reasonable" price, which is influenced both by the prices of the competition and also by actual funds available. Many would-be authors or journal editors claim that there is no competition: they are almost always wrong. Even if unusually the author is correct in his or her claim, the obvious question for the publisher to ask is why no-one has filled the gap before. Projected books or serials should always be carefully planned and the plans then carried through to the actual publication. Costs should be contained so that a price can be set at a level that fits in with what the market will tolerate. A common problem in book publishing is an author who writes too much or, who tries to insist on too many illustrations. If an author asked to write a textbook running to (say) 300 pages produces a manuscript running to 1000 pages, it should be sent back for shortening. It is better to do that than either produce a book that is going to be too expensive when it is priced or taking a loss on the enterprise. A budget for a journal has to be set at the time, at least six months before the year of publication, in order that a journal subscription rate can be set. Costs depend mostly on the number of pages published in a year and it is most important that the editor of the journal is involved in budgetary calculations and understands the impact of what is decided on the editorial process. If too many accepted articles build up you have a choice between increasing the page budget and inevitably the subscription price of the journal or insisting upon a higher rejection rate.

5.6.3   Announcement of prices

Some publishers announce book prices before the manuscript is in house and revise the announcement when publication gets nearer but this is not good practice. It causes problems to the book trade and to agents representing the programme. Prices announced should be firm prices. The rates of subscription to journals should be announced by June/July in the year previous to that of the volume concerned and particular care should be taken to inform the main subscription agents immediately. There is a growing tendency to adopt one price throughout the world expressed in one major currency, as well as a local rate if this is appropriate. Any extra charges for postage should always be made clear.

5.7   Print runs

The setting of an appropriate print run is particularly important for books. Printing more journals than is needed for subscribers is often done as the issues left over can be used as samples. With books there is always a tendency among publishers to print too many because most book printers give much lower unit costs for longer print runs. It is almost always best practice to print too few copies of a book rather than too many, especially as printing on demand is becoming ever cheaper and of better quality. Journal print-runs are easier to project but with journals there is a tendency among publishers to under-print usually through not taking into account sufficiently the number of issues given away as samples. It is expensive to go back to press but important to have a stock of complete volumes, especially when the journal is not mature, because libraries often wish to buy complete volumes.

CHAPTER 6
PRODUCTION AND PRESENTATION

A lot of money is spent on production and not always wisely. In this chapter four areas have been concentrated on. Copy-editing is part of the value-added rationale for publishers mentioned in chapter 2. Although some learned societies do all their production in house, most look for suppliers whether typesetters, printers or binders. Criteria for choosing are crucial. The look of the product is also very important and there is a whole range of standards, conventions and practices which may make the difference, in some cases to the content being retrievable or not. The production and presentation demands of going online have already been outlined in chapter 3.

6.1   Copy-editing

Copy-editing is an important part of the value added by learned societies. There are levels of copy-editing with more intervention involving more expertise and probably more cost. Starting at the simplest interpretation of what the term means, copy-editing can mean marking up for the printer in accordance with a house style. This is a relatively straightforward exercise. Ensuring the accuracy of grammar, punctuation, and spelling is also part of standard procedures. Copy-editing can also imply checking that units are consistently used, that references are complete (and sometimes checking that they are accurate) and that all figures are complete and appropriately referred to. It usually involves making arguments clear where there is a lack of clarity of expression. It sometimes covers in addition serious work on the text where the author does not have English as a first language. These last two functions are particularly worth undertaking for a member of the ICSU family because they offer a service of importance for scholarship, which (alas) is now rarely available from commercial publishers. The society publisher will have to come to a view on what level of copy-editing it is offering and whether it is to be done in-house or outsourced.

6.2   Choosing and working with a supplier.

6.2.1   The importance of the decisions made

Production represents the biggest bills incurred by the publisher but often decisions are not made with the same care as editorial and marketing decisions are made, partly because of the perceived specialist nature of the print-buying process. Quite a number of learned societies do their typesetting in house, though in this chapter it is assumed that an outside supplier is used, but almost all use such suppliers for printing and binding. There are some simple rules that can be understood by non-specialists. It is appropriate to add here that the term "supplier" is used throughout rather than "printer" because printing and "typesetting" (or "composition") are often handled by different companies as indeed may be the case for colour artwork.

6.2.2   The functions that may be outsourced

The publisher may need the following functions performed by an external company. For books these are the production of a text design, the design of a cover or jacket, the typesetting or proofing of the book, the printing, the choice of paper, the binding, and possibly even distribution, warehousing and fulfilment of orders. To this list may be added copy-editing. The list is much the same for journals.

6.2.3   Interfacing

Even if some of these functions are performed in house the interface between the other functions has to be considered. For example when a learned society copy-edits and typesets a book or journal in-house it must liaise closely with the printer. It is important to arrange schedules that interlock and are treated seriously. Suppliers do not hold machines or staff members in readiness for the customer to give them their material at the time which suits the customer. They have to allocate time in advance. It is also imperative that the final output going to printers (camera-ready copy, PostScript or PDF files) suits the way the printer works, and that the way illustrations are handled results in the most appropriate quality in the finished item. The way in which the medical reader expects an X-ray to appear on a finished page is very different from what the geologist expects from a landscape illustration in one of his or her books.

6.2.4   Specialisation among suppliers

The difference between the ways in which a supplier handles books and journals comes down to the different schedules required. Journals have fixed schedules and recur in accordance with a regular timetable. Books can usually be fitted in. Suppliers charge less page by page for book production than they do for journal production. Different typesetters tend to specialise in one type of publishing or the other. It is also more important to have a long-standing relationship for a journal where there is a continuous flow of material needing the same treatment to produce the same appearance, whereas each book in most cases, though not necessarily with a series, can be treated as a one-off item. It is also important to remember that small companies that usually do stationery are not good choices for learned journals; similarly, printers specialising in large volume colour work are not appropriate for scholarly monographs with a few colour plates.

6.2.5   Working with one or several suppliers

In all cases a relationship where each party knows each other's procedures is of great advantage particularly where the publishing party is relatively small. Suppliers that can handle the whole process are to be sought in these circumstances. Larger publishers tend to work with a different printer from their typesetter and there are also cost advantages in working with a paper merchant to buy the most appropriate paper rather than using the stock bought in and regularly used by the printer. If different suppliers are used for different stages in the publishing process it is crucial that they fit together well. This is a much more complex procedure in the electronic environment.

6.2.6   How to choose a supplier

Given this background to the process of choosing, how does one choose? In the first place choose suppliers that already do the sort of work that you want them to quote for. Ask to see samples of work already being done for another client. Book typesetters that do not handle journals often think they are able to do so with ease: do not accept this contention. Half-tone photographs that require high resolution, medical illustrations such as X-rays and mathematics setting where four-line equations are required: all these prerequisites come under a general recommendation of making sure that the supplier can handle what the publisher wants, to an appropriate standard and schedule, and cost-effectively,.

6.2.7 Knowing and communicating what is required

It is also crucial that the supplier is told exactly what is wanted. For a book the request for a costing should include: the probable number of pages in the book; a representative sample of the typescript and/or an example of the electronic format likely to be delivered; the type of paper required with ideally an example; information about the illustration content – how many photographs, line-drawings etc., the style of binding; the number of colours for the binding or cover etc. etc. The rule is that the more detail given to the supplier the more realistic the quote will be. However an insistence by the society on particular requirements, for example, a specific type of paper is not always the best plan: there are good reasons to leave space for advice to be given by the supplier about possibly cheaper alternative approaches. The situation for a journal is much the same but some of the decisions are even more important because it is about a standard of appearance that may last for years and a schedule that may be crucial to the journal getting off the ground. What the first issue of a journal looks like is important for selling subscriptions and encouraging authors to submit articles. With a journal the schedule should be outlined by the prospective supplier and in particular the publisher must make sure that enough time is allowed for the authors of articles to receive and return their proofs. At the same time, where the journal is new, flexibility in the supplier is needed because shortage of copy for early issues may lead to publishers asking the supplier to do their part of the job quicker than was agreed. There are special circumstances relating to the production of electronic files which have been touched on in section 3.5.

6.2.8 How suppliers charge

Different suppliers present costs in different ways. For example a price per page given by a typesetter may look very competitive but less obvious may be the very high charges for changes in proof. For printers carriage costs must be made clear. It is important to be aware of what additional charges there will be if there are variations asked for subsequent to an agreement being reached. Make sure too that all costs are shown and that this and all other parts of the quotation are in writing.

A good relationship and one of mutual trust is of prime importance.

6.3 Appropriate presentation.

6.3.1 Appearance

Publishers aiming to reach a particular audience should make sure that their publication looks "normal" to that audience. The urge to develop a distinctive design is often strong in smaller companies and should be resisted if the audience is to instinctively trust what they see as apparently authoritative and relevant. It is worth taking into account the sort of image projected by the books or journals produced by the those publishing companies that are the most visible in the discipline concerned.

6.3.2 Conventions

The same principle is relevant when considering conventions relating to references or units in the text of the book or article. A "house style" may well be appropriate for one discipline but not for another. It is not a good idea to insist on particular conventions being adopted by an author, which may not be the norm in his or her community. There is no point also in changing one valid spelling for another. Who provides the standards varies from discipline to discipline but a good starting point, if there is any doubt, is the list of international unions provided on the main ICSU site, the URL of which is given in the Preface.

6.4 Standards and conventions

6.4.1 Best practice

This sub-section can only touch on the range of standards and conventions that apply to book and journal publishing. There is a lot of literature available on standards, some of which has been pointed to in section 3.7 where they apply to electronic publishing. Some of the URLs quoted are relevant to print publishing. The central organisation concerned with such matters is the International Organization for Standardization, 1, rue de Varembe, Case postale 56, CH-1211 Geneva 20, Switzerland. It can provide the name and address of the relevant local organisation. The emphasis of the subsections below is on practical implementation. There is not a straightforward distinction between standards and conventions: best practice or good practice perhaps better describes the content of this part of the

Guidelines. Specifically, as far as conventions are concerned, there is no attempt here to go into layout, the way in which the page is designed. For both books and journals there is everything to be gained, as the communication of science is the aim, by presenting the content on the page in a way which is clear, straightforward and appropriate.

6.4.2 Standing matter

The material that is included at the front and back of every journal issue is known as "standing matter". It includes guidance for authors (which are mentioned below) and also information about ordering. Some of the components of the standing matters are now described. Some of the sources already mentioned provide check-lists and an invaluable pamphlet is *Serial Publications: Guidelines for Good Practice in Publishing Printed Journals and other Serial Publications.* Clearly this deals with journals only: it is available from the United Kingdom Serials Group, 114, Woodstock Road, Witney OX8 6DY United Kingdom. It is intended that this guide will be revised in the near future.

6.4.3 International standard numbers

It is very important to apply for an international standard serial number (ISSN) if the publication is a journal and to allocate an international standard book number (ISBN) if a book. The absence of these standard numbers means that a publication is almost impossible to find outside your own country. The systems work rather differently. There is an international centre for the ISSN at www.issn.org pointing to the relevant local agency but there is no such resource for the ISBN. The International ISBN Agency does nevertheless have an email address i.e. ISBN@SBB.SPK-Berlin.de which can be consulted. Otherwise it is best to turn to the national library for assistance.

6.4.4 Cataloguing in Publication

Another item of information, intended also to help retrieval of information about a book title, is the recording in a book of Cataloguing in Publication (CIP) data. The data includes the full name of the author or editor, the full title and sub-title, the name of the translator if there is one, the places of publication with the principal one given first, the name of the publisher and the date of publication. CIP schemes provide for standard national catalogue information to be printed on the verso of the title pages of books (see below). They speed the listing of books in national bibliographies and thus make it possible for orders to reach the publisher early. The publisher should send either the preliminary matter for, or complete proofs of, forthcoming titles to their local CIP centre. There is no international listing of these centres and, again, the best place to get information on such schemes is the national library. For countries with such schemes it is not customary now to actually list all the information but rather to refer to the data lodged with the national bibliography. However in countries where no scheme exists it is nevertheless worth listing the same sort of information on the verso of the title page.

6.4.5 The title

It should be obvious that a clear, descriptive and relevant title is essential for a book or a journal. Nevertheless design considerations and lack of attention mean that rather too frequently titles are only given in part or not set out clearly on cover or jacket and, in the case of serials, modified without warning or need. There is an excellent four page pamphlet on titles, and other matters including bar codes (essential for books and worthwhile for journals) from the Library of Congress entitled "What's in a Name?". The URL is : lcweb.loc.gov/issn/whats.html.

6.4.6 Book title pages and covers

Books should carry the title, subtitle (if any), series (if any) author/ editor and publisher on the title page and outside front cover. In addition the title page should give the year of publication. If the spine is wide enough, author, title (abbreviated if necessary) and publisher should be printed on it. English language publishers characteristically run the wording downward along the spine should this be necessary. The ISBN should appear on the outside back cover and/or jacket ideally in the bottom right hand corner and in both numerical and bar code form if possible. The back of the title page is customarily known as the verso, or copyright page. This page should carry: the address of the publisher; a copyright line and associated information (see section 4.2.4 above); the date of first publication and those of reprints or new editions; the country in which the book was printed and (in some jurisdictions) the name and address of the printer; CIP data if available; and the ISBN.

6.4.7   Journal title pages and covers

There is a convention about what should go on the cover and on the title page of journal issues which is set out in the UKSG pamphlet cited in section 6.4.2. Contents may be given on the front or back covers or on the title page and it is helpful if the title page, which is often photocopied for retrieval purposes, presents, as well as a list of contents the title, volume and part or issue number, date of publication and ISSN and the name of the publisher. There is a growing practice of giving the copyright line both on the title page and also on the opening of each new article: this to make sure that the journal is identified when copies of the individual article are circulated or made available separately. If possible the spine of the issue should give the title of the journal, the volume and issue numbers, the pagination of that issue, and the date of publication, running downwards from top to bottom. A volume title page and verso page, organised as for a book, should be provided along with an index either with the last issue of the volume or the first issue of a new volume.

CHAPTER 7
INSTRUCTING THE AUTHOR

7.1   How to instruct

This chapter is written from the point of view of the publisher. All publishers issue instructions to (or, as some prefer, guidance for) their journal contributors and to their volume authors and editors as to how they would wish their material to be prepared. Different houses have different styles but there are key features of all which can be mentioned here. In the case of journals, the instructions to authors are usually part of the standing matter of (preferably) each issue, but with books they tend to be sent out with contracts or as part of the instructions given to presenters of papers at symposia. Among the general points that can be made are the following. Be clear and simple. Do not specify style too closely but be appropriate (see section 6.3). Finally a practical point may be worth making: if the instructions are prepared separately make them large format as small format documents tend to fall to the bottom of files and be mislaid. It is now common to make such documents available on the website of a publisher which makes it much easier for authors to access them and publishers to keep them up to date.

7.2   Format

7.2.1   The use of discs

When the term "electronic publishing" began to come into use the initial practical impact for publishers was that it enabled them to receive content from authors on disc as well as on paper. This has already been mentioned in section 3.5.1 earlier in these Guidelines. The significant cost-savings projected at the time have only partially been realised because of the large range of formats used by authors. Nevertheless most publishers find it well worthwhile trying to get their authors to hand over a disc as well as the hard copy generated by the word processor and some publishers insist on it. The advantage for the authors is that it may be possible to avoid re-keying and thus unnecessary alteration of what they have written. It is sensible to offer a template or style sheets particularly for a journal and make it available on a website. If instructions have to be given in hard copy form it is the systems of headings and the reference system which are most important to specify, other than the handling of illustrations which is touched on below.

7.2.2   Specifications

The publisher should specify the nature of the discs that they can handle including the version of the software. Currently (1999) Word files are the most likely deliverables which most can manage. Many mathematicians and those disciplines using a lot of mathematics use varieties of TeX, most commonly LaTeX. Chemists often favour Macintosh software. The format requested should be what the community concerned uses most frequently. Hard copy should always be requested too but, as part of the instructions, it must be established from the start which version (disc or hardcopy) is to be regarded as normative. Whatever is decided, a decision should be made with regard to the way in which both the refereeing and the copy-editing are to be handled. If it is intended that the discs are delivered to the typesetter (whether an internal or an external function) the capabilities of the system used must be ascertained and taken into account. The cost advantages of using author-generated discs and the benefits of not having to ask an author to check proofs may be nullified if there is a technological mismatch leading to a need to re-key.

7.2.3   The use of abstracts

Abstracts are required at the head of all journal articles, because secondary publishers that facilitate retrieval of the article need them. They also feature at the start of many book chapters. Instructions should be given according to the custom in the discipline concerned.

7.3   Illustrations

7.3.1   The handling of illustrations

In science publishing the handling of illustrations is a major cause of confusion and resulting friction between author and publisher. Publishers usually expect authors to supply illustrations in a form ready for immediate use complete with any labelling and lettering. It is very important that the percentage reduction to be used in the production process is made clear so that the author can size the lettering accordingly and that the lines can be of an appropriate thickness. In certain disciplines, information about the resolution (dots per inch) adopted in graphic files should be provided by the publisher for the author. It is also important that the form in which line drawings, graphs etc. are to be presented should be specified in line with current practice. A glance at many instructions to authors reveals that in this area the instructions are often not in accord with actual practice. Publishers should never ask their authors to do unnecessary work. A wide range of powerful artwork software is available and this fact should be taken into account.

7.3.2 Half tone and colour photographs

Black and white photographs (half tones), which must be originals, are usually easy to handle though special instructions should be given for some medical illustrations such as X-rays. The publisher must come to a view on colour plates. They are expensive to reproduce and many publishers ask for grants to cover the extra costs. Clear instructions need to be given. It is important to make clear that the published version cannot be of higher quality than the originals. Sometimes illustrations are presented which the publisher needs to crop and in this case the point being illustrated must be made clear. Special instructions about captions also need to be given. Because illustrations are often retrieved out of context, the explanation of its significance in the caption should be explicit without reference to the article in which the illustration is embedded.

7.4 Rights

Instructions to authors should always include information about the publishing policy of the journal with regard to material previously made public either by being previously published or, in the case of journals, being made available on an open website. In the case of both books and journals the form in which permission to use copyright material is to be obtained must be specified. These questions are dealt with at greater length in section 4.3.

CHAPTER 8
DISTRIBUTION AND MARKETING

It is usually relatively easy for the smaller publisher to handle the production of books or journals but if the intention is to reach the international audience in particular, distribution and marketing are more of a problem. Distribution questions including order fulfilment are therefore covered first. Marketing in its full sense including market research is part of the value-added services supplied by the publisher. In this chapter however marketing is used as synonymous with promotion and promotion as described is based on traditional techniques. The opportunities presented by the Internet, which are only now beginning to be properly explored, have already been touched on in section 3.6.4. One further point needs to be made here. Promotion is not just intended to sell the publication to a purchaser. It is intended also to sell the publication to a prospective author in the case of a journal or a book series and indeed to sell the publisher itself to the community it is trying to serve.

8.1   Selling and distribution

8.1.1   Journal fulfilment and distribution
The handling of journal subscriptions is not difficult to accomplish from one centre for the whole world. The actual distribution, given close cooperation with local postal authorities either directly or through mailing houses, is not one of the greatest problems for the smaller company. There are lots of commercial companies that provide consolidation services that can save a lot of money on postage. These services operate by gaining lower prices from the postal authorities as a reward for grouping together items intended for the same destination. Subscriptions to journals from libraries are usually mediated through subscription agents, and most of the business goes through a small number of really big companies that are very professional at working with publishers in whatever country. Libraries prefer to work with agents that save them money by presenting them with a single invoice rather than their getting one for each publisher and also providing a whole range of services, traditionally claiming missing issues but now also comprising even core library functions such as cataloguing.

8.1.2   Book distribution and representation

Books often present more of a problem. It is traditional to arrange for representation to bookshops in the main markets where it is hoped the publication concerned will be bought. Sales managers often set up a network of agents to accomplish this purpose. It is not at all clear that it is cost-effective to spend much time and money, particularly on international travel, to establish and maintain these sorts of arrangements. Bookshops do not stock most academic publications but it is important of course that they can find information about the book in the appropriate directories (see section 8.1.3 below). Unfortunately in spite of the existence of some really international wholesalers, in key markets such as North America, libraries characteristically work through book vendors which are reluctant to buy from outside a small number of countries not including some major publishing nations. Sometimes (but rarely) it is possible to find a co-publisher in the USA, particularly from among the ranks of the many excellent university presses: such an arrangement can include an investment in costs. Usually however a distribution deal is the answer, but the arrangement does not need to cover much more than stocking, handling orders and, above all, providing a local address, though it can if required include local marketing. In either case, the other party has to cover its costs and make a profit from the discount given. The discount given by the publisher to the agents will vary a great deal depending on the range of services offered and whether the sale is direct or through a bookseller or other intermediary.

8.1.3   Directories

For journals it is essential that there is an entry in *Ulrich's International Periodicals Directory*, which is available from the publisher R.R.Bowker, 121 Chanlon Road, New Providence, NJ 07974 USA. It is also available online and to find out more see www.reedref.com. Mention should also be made of Publist billed as the Internet Directory of Publications and which deals with both books and journals. To find out how to obtain an entry go to their website – www.publist.com. For books each major publishing nation has its own directory. In the USA Books in Print is produced by the Bowker company also: it is available through a range of electronic outlets as well as in print. In the UK the equivalent publication is published by Whitakers at 12, Dyott Street, London WC1A 1DF. A distribution address in either market can make coverage in either of these directories possible. English language titles published in Africa, Asia, Australia, Canada, Continental Europe, Latin America, New Zealand, Oceania and the Republic of Ireland are listed in *International Books in Print* published by K.G.Saur Verlag, Ortlerstrasse 8, D-81373 München, Germany (www.saur.de).

8.2 Order fulfilment

Mention has already been made in the section on publishing finance of the importance of getting purchasers to pay for publications as soon as possible. It is crucial that the learned society organises its financial arrangements to encompass order fulfilment, which may involve putting in new systems to handle international transactions. Sometimes such services are best handled by other companies that include larger publishers. There are significant economies of scale particular where journals are concerned. The small publisher does not need to lose its identity by taking advantage of such arrangements as they are customarily tailored to permit such facilities as invoicing using your own letterhead.

8.3 Direct mail promotion

8.3.1 Costs

This is the usual method of selling academic publications. It is not cheap; a rough rule of thumb is that direct costs will be about double the costs of postage. These calculations also assume that you have access to mailing lists of potential purchasers of the book or journal. In either case the purchaser may well be a library but their buying decisions are influenced by pressure from patrons or users. In the case of journals and costly books like encyclopaedias, it may be worth mailing libraries directly (see section 8.6 below).

8.3.2 Mailing lists

Publishers do not always recognise that they already hold a number of useful lists themselves including the record of their customers, and their authors including authors of journal articles. There are three other main sources of mailing lists: your own authors or editors, other learned societies and list brokers. If pressed, authors or editors or (in the case of journals) editorial boards can often provide some very useful lists of specialist groups, and learned societies to which they belong. These lists are invaluable but make sure that the donor has permission to give them away for the purpose intended. In a growing number of jurisdictions data protection legislation has to be taken into account. Other learned societies may be willing to help but they are sometimes very reluctant to let their lists leave their buildings and their charges for doing a mailing themselves may be quite high. There are some good list brokers mainly in the USA but they are expensive. Always make sure that you do not send out a lot of leaflets to lists that are too broad in coverage: this is not cost-effective.

8.3.3   Writing promotional material

Promotional material need not be elaborate. It should include all the basic bibliographical information including ISSN or ISBN, the name and address of the publisher and/or the address for orders, and the price. The description of the book or journal (the "blurb") should be informative rather than eulogistic: a list of contents is more valuable than something written by a publisher. There is however always a place for a commendation by a well-known academic, particularly one well known in a key market like North America. In the case of a journal there is a lot to be gained by listing a prestigious editorial board.

8.4   Advertising

Every survey of buying habits among academics or librarians shows that response to what is called "space advertising" is low on the list of reasons for purchase. It can also be expensive. Nevertheless a small publisher wishing to sell a new journal to a wide international audience may consider that the investment of their marketing budget in, for example, a full page advertisement in a journal like *Nature*, which reaches the majority of biomedical researchers, could be worth the purchase cost. It might be better than using a large number of big mailing lists for much the same overall expenditure. Advertisements in society newsletters may be a cheaper way of reaching the membership than using their mailing service. Information included in the advertisement is much the same as proposed for mailing pieces. It is worth considering exchanging advertisements with other relevant publications or in the mailings of other learned societies.

8.5 Exhibitions

It is crucial for the success of a book or journal that the person who will recommend its purpose sees an inspection or sample copy. Whereas sample copies of journals can now be got not only by post but also from the sites of the publisher where the trend is to make sample issues freely available, book vendors and wholesalers are increasingly reluctant to send out books on approval. Specialist conferences are therefore very important as they often present opportunities for the display of publications. Hiring a stand and manning it is too expensive for the smaller publisher in most cases but co-operative exhibitions often make it possible to have a display. The conference organisers will often give information about such services

8.6 Using intermediaries

Subscription agents can be very helpful in letting libraries know about new journals. The big ones offer various promotional services including the creation of highly targeted lists. The big four (Blackwells, Dawson/Faxon, EBSCO, and Swets) have extensive websites which explain how these services can be accessed. It is crucial to make sure that a new journal is held in their databases. A wider range of intermediaries including services owned by some publishers themselves and one library organisation (OCLC) help publishers bring their online publications more effectively to the libraries and, through the libraries, to the individual scientists. Each intermediary has its own offering of publications fronted by an interface. Usually the intermediary links through to the content on the publisher's server or the server which otherwise hosts the publications but some offer to act as a host themselves. There is no consensus among publishers about how to view such organisations but in general it is true to say that at the present time suspicion is mainly found among the very big publishers whereas smaller companies are only too pleased by the added exposure such offerings bring to their publications.

8.7 Abstracting and indexing services

8.7.1 Use where worth using

These secondary services are much used by scholars and can direct them to your publication. Almost all cater for particular disciplines and it is therefore not appropriate to list them all. Learned societies will naturally know which companies are appropriate to contact. Most are concerned primarily with journal articles, but some also cover multi-authored books including symposium proceedings. Some will buy your journal or book but many expect to receive free copies. Never send copies without checking in advance that they are going to be used and review your "gratis" list regularly or you can find out that you have a big postage bill for very little benefit.

8.7.2 The Institute of Scientific Information

Which secondary services you approach will depend on the discipline of your publication, except in the case of the Institute of Scientific Information's Current Contents service. For journals, to be in *Current Contents* is a major advantage. The number of journals covered remains fairly constant and decisions are made by international review bodies of scholars. It is recommended that publishers should submit one copy of the first issue of a journal they would like evaluated immediately upon publication. This should be sent to Editorial Development – ISI, 3501 Market Street, Philadelphia, PA 19104, USA. A letter should accompany the issue explaining the aims and scope of the journal and giving a contact name. At least the first three issues of a new journal must be reviewed before a coverage decision can be made, so the second and third issues should also be sent to the same address as they are published. It is crucial to acceptance into this service, and many others, that the journal is published on schedule.

8.8 Review copies

A good review of a book in a periodical read by your target audience can make a great deal of difference to sales. When drawing up a list of journals or magazines to which review copies should be sent, check that they actually cover reviews. The information on this point is to be found in *Ulrich* (cited earlier in section 8.1.3). For expensive publications it is worth checking in advance that the book fits in with the reviewing policy of the periodical. Make sure that you send full details of the book including the address for orders. Not many periodicals review journals on a routine basis but *Nature* does so twice a year. Check when the next journals issue is due and the criteria for and timing of submission.

8.9 Legal deposit

Many countries have passed legislation placing an obligation on publishers to provide free of charge to designated libraries copies of printed books and journals that they publish and there is a movement to extend "legal deposit" to electronic/digital materials. There is no accessible international listing of the practices in different countries and the best advice is to check with the national library to find out what has to be done.

CHAPTER 9
WORKING WITH A PARTNER

In much of the previous sections of these guidelines the assumption has been that the learned society is handling its own publishing, perhaps with some outsourcing of specialist functions or with some collaboration over, for example, distribution. Guidance is particularly necessary for societies going it alone because, if you are working with a partner, much of the information included in these sections is familiar to the (larger) partner. Part of the relationship should always be to give general publishing advice on the range of issues that come up.

9.1   Why seek a partner?

Many societies decide that their publishing programmes will be more secure and that the income flow will be more reliable if they partner with another publisher who will have a larger programme and staff already in place covering all publishing functions. There can obviously be economies of scale. In the case of start-ups the investment required can come from another rather than from the society itself. The problems associated with electronic publishing demand expertise that is expensive and difficult to secure but which may already exist within a prospective partner. Essentially learned society publishers may feel that they do a better job for their authors and their members by entering into such a relationship (see section 9.2).

9.2   Deciding what is wanted

Before a partner is sought and before substantive negotiations are entered into, it is appropriate for a learned society to decide what they want from the relationship. This will be dependent on the nature of the publication, the funds available, and the amount of control that the learned society wishes to exercise over the operation. Ownership is important and is considered below.

9.2.1 Partnering with a company/organisation which is not a publisher

In what follows it is assumed that the partner is another publisher. In the area of journal publishing there have been printers who offer a "full service" extending to marketing and subscription fulfilment but they have not found it possible to invest in those parts of the publishing role outside their core business areas to an extent that convinces potential customers. In the electronic arena there are some companies which offer a range of services involving subscription fulfilment and distribution and even the production of electronic files, an extension of what is offered by the electronic hosts mentioned in chapter 3. If you want to outsource that range of services, these offerings are worth considering

9.2.2 Non-profit or profit

Committees of learned societies that decide to work with a partner often have members with strong views about whether that partner should be another learned society or a commercial publisher. In fact there is no straight antithesis between profit and non-profit. Most big learned society or university presses are operationally identical and hold policies, for example on copyright, which are indistinguishable from those commercial publishers. All parties wish to make a surplus or profit and will view any relationship with a client society accordingly. It is also not appropriate to view all commercial publishers in the same way. Some companies specialise in working with learned societies and are willing to take a lower profit margin in order to secure such relationships and the larger turnover involved. However it is the case that any surplus a learned society makes is ploughed back into the discipline, or, in the case of a university press, back into the university, whereas the profits of a commercial house go to the shareholders: this may be seen as significant.

9.2.3 The quality of the relationship

It is not always best to go for the biggest. The various economies of scale in a larger house should be weighed against the specialised talents of a smaller house. It is not uncommon for a relationship to break down because a learned society finds no single champion but a succession of employees in different functions dealing with their business. Part of the deal can be for a single responsible person being assigned to the job of liaising, though of course even in such circumstances staff turnover cannot be prevented.

9.3   How to choose a partner

9.3.1   The establishment of criteria

On the assumption that the learned society approaches the search for a partner with a clear remit, there are a number of criteria to be considered. These should be explicitly listed: indeed there is a strong case for producing a tender document which should be sent out to prospective partners, requiring a formal response and followed by a formal interview to discuss the answers in detail. There is every reason for negotiating until the best partner has been identified: a structured approach prevents a charming individual presenting and having accepted an over-optimistic scenario, or existing relationships between a particular house and officers of the society being given too much weight. Obviously an agreement over a single book, for example a symposium proceedings, does not warrant spending so much time on negotiation but the transfer or starting of a series of books or a journal require much the same level of attention and much the same criteria can be used.

9.3.2   The publishing programme of the potential partner.

The publisher considered should normally have an active list of proven books and journals in the field of study or discipline in question. If a journal is under consideration it is not a good idea to enter into a relationship with a publisher that specialises in books. A decent list of reasonable size, already well known, will have given the publisher credibility with booksellers or agents and also an image with potential buyers that will already know and respect the imprint. Undoubtedly the existence on the partner's list of an active programme in a relevant area enables greater marketing penetration through mailings which are cost-effective because they can include a larger number of titles. The same goes for sectional catalogues and, in particular, justifies a presence at exhibitions. Members of a learned society deputed to negotiate with a projected partner may know from their own experience how well that company handled their own publications. Catalogues reveal pricing policies, which may be important, and the size and breadth of the distribution network. Visits to local bookshops and even casual conversations with bookshop staff can be informative.

9.3.3 Questions of production quality and schedules

Examination of their books or journals will reveal what sort of production standards the prospective partner has. They need to have the ability to handle and print the type of material the publishing society has in mind. This is particularly true where mathematics setting is concerned or where there is a high incidence of quality half-tone photographs. It is not possible to tell from the publication in its finished form whether the publisher had internal systems capable of, for example, handling discs from author or from the society itself but detailed questions can and should be asked. There is also the question of schedules. In the case of journals the gap between acceptance and publication dates in the journal itself reveal a lot but direct questioning may be needed to establish how long it takes for a book to be published after submission of the final text.

9.3.4 One partner or several?

The learned society needs to be sure that the partner is efficient and has acceptable policies and that these efficiencies and policies can be demonstrated practically and not just in paper presentations or in words at meetings. Many societies with extensive publishing programmes prefer to work with one publishing company but others will have relationships with several. This preference is partly because different partners are seen as more appropriate for different sections of the programme; but also for strategic reasons – to minimise the dangers of too great a reliance being placed on one party.

9.4 The contract with a partner

This section is not concerned with outlining the arrangement of the contractual document and the topics considered are not listed in the order in which they would customarily be treated in a contract. The range of relationships that are possible is too great for a template to be drawn up which would be more useful than misleading.

9.4.1 What each party brings to the relationship

Basically the society brings to a relationship its prestige, its members and its ability to attract authors and contributors, often from its ranks. It may offer its membership as potential or, in the case of a journal, actual purchasers – sometimes as part of their membership subscription. It also brings to the publishing partner extra revenue and profits and more visibility. The partner offers its publishing expertise and experience and all the advantages that flow from this. Some contracts outline these types of statements in a preamble.

9.4.2 Types of financial arrangements

The contract with a partner is built around the basic financial arrangement. There are three main types: a commission arrangement, a royalty arrangement and a profit sharing arrangement. As relationships they are ranked in ascending order of closeness between society and partner and they will be treated in this order.

9.4.3 Commission arrangements

A commission arrangement is when the learned society pays a publishing partner a commission, usually a percentage of revenue received from sales, for performing a number of specified functions such as sales and marketing, order/subscription fulfilment and warehousing and distribution. The publishing partner deducts the money received under this arrangement from the income that comes in and passes what remains on to the society. Just occasionally it is the other way round. In such an arrangement production bills are usually paid by the society. For such an arrangement to be feasible the society must have the money to invest. The society pays directly but at the same time exerts more or less total control. The biggest drawback, apart from the financial risk and possibly poor cash-flow involved, is that the society may not take advantage of offering the whole range of services that are involved in the publishing business. It thus misses out on the sort of help a bigger and more experienced company may be able to give. This may now be a more important consideration than it was, in view of the rapid changes and opportunities presented by the Internet. There is also little incentive for the publisher to do more than is absolutely necessary for the society.

9.4.4 Royalty and profit-sharing arrangements

Royalty and profit-sharing arrangements both assume the publishing partner providing the investment and suffering the risk. Royalties on income from sales are attractive to a society starting new projects as they kick in from the beginning. They are also easy to interpret and to check. Profit sharing is preferable in a situation where there is a mature list of publications and in particular where journals are involved. Some societies wisely ask for both arrangements to be calculated and ask to be paid on whichever basis gives them the most money. Profit-sharing needs to be very carefully set out in contractual terms. There are many different ways of doing this, some of which involve calculations that are impossible to check. Any such calculations are to be avoided. Perhaps the most satisfactory definition of profits is one in which costs of production and marketing and perhaps some other functions which can be demonstrated by invoices from external suppliers plus an overhead charge, is deducted from revenue. The trouble is that the overhead charge, though possible to define as a percentage of revenue, cannot be justified in any way that can be checked. Why 25% from one company and 15% from another? A variant of profit-sharing is a joint account arrangement where the society and the publisher both allocate their specified costs and the profit represents the revenue after these costs have been deducted. The revenue also has to be defined closely: in the case of a journal is it revenue from subscription income or subscriptions plus subsidiary rights income plus advertising revenue? Does it also include revenue from offprints, reprints or royalty fees from document delivery? It is easiest to specify "all revenue".

9.4.5 Other financial considerations

It can be argued that any arrangement, which does not encourage the partner to work harder to do better financially, will not result in the most successful publication. There is no point assuming the worst of what is intended to be a mutually beneficial arrangement. However the society should not get too close. It should always insist on clarity and a formula which allows checking. It is important always to insist that the financial records of the company, the "books", which relate to the society's publishing, are open to inspection.

9.4.6 Other contractual clauses

The other parts of the contract should cover much the same areas as the contracts with authors/editors described in outline in section 4.1

and for journals given as in Appendix 2. There are obvious differences in that detailed arrangements for schedules for individual projects are not best dealt with in an agreement covering an overall relationship. Clauses specifically covering arrangements related to electronic publishing are mentioned below in section 9.5.

9.4.7 Ownership

Ownership is crucial especially in the case of journals, where many societies think that they own a journal but find that it can be taken away from them. Any contract must be explicit concerning ownership, which includes not only the title but also the subscription list and also (if wished) the back issues or, in the case of books, the inventory. The publishing partner should be obligated to obtain an assignment of copyright on behalf of the society and the copyright line of the society should be prominently displayed.

9.4.8 Editorial control

Societies normally wish to have some if not total editorial control. They worry that the publisher will try to take this away. However this anxiety is almost always unfounded. Publishers usually want the society partner to take an active part in the editing and validation of content. They may however insist on a final veto for commercial or legal reasons in order to protect their investment. This should be spelt out clearly in the agreement

9.4.9 Handling of rights

Many societies find it easier for downstream rights (as defined in the introduction to chapter 4) to be handled by the publisher especially in view of the complexities now existing in the electronic environment – in return for a share of the income. In the case of upstream rights societies are usually happy that the partner use its standard contractual arrangements with authors, editors and contributors with, if necessary, small alterations only. In such cases the society should be clear about the partner's policies and practices. The contracts themselves can be an addendum to the main agreement between the two parties.

9.4.10 Pricing policies

The same goes for pricing policies. Individual books may be priced by the publishing partner at its discretion within an agreed range but it is sensible to make sure that journal pricing must be agreed. If the deal over a journal includes a supply to members at a reduced fee, this rate must be under the control of the society.

9.4.11 Membership obligations

There are a number of ways of dealing with the society's obligations to its members. Some societies make their journals available to members as part of the subscription. Sometimes there is a choice between a number of journals, if the society publishes several journals. Sometimes the society asks members to pay for any publications, presenting payment as an option on membership forms but at a considerable discount. In a deal with the publishing partner, the partner may distribute these copies without charge to the society, or charge postage or charge a sum per member supplied. Depending on the complexities of the societies publishing arrangements, there can be some difficult calculations here to make sure that the society makes the best bargain.

9.4.12 Production questions

Editorial control by the society sometimes extends to the provision of in-house typesetting services and the delivery of camera ready copy or a disc: in this case the obligation to maintain a level of quality and an adherence to schedules could be asked of the society by the partner. In most cases societies are in a position of wanting to make sure that their publications come out in reasonable time and that standards of production are as felt appropriate. There is often surprising difficulty in getting publishers to follow a particular style or format that the society has decided upon. The colour of the binding and the typography on the spine are examples of aspects of the production process curiously difficult to pin down. Societies can reasonably ask that production standards be guaranteed in contracts: this can be defined by reference to a specific book or journal.

9.4.13 Marketing questions

Questions about the level of marketing are often an important feature of tender documents but promises about marketing made by publishing partners at that stage almost always disappoint in reality and can become a major cause of friction. One way of minimising the gap between hope and reality is to tie the partner to a level of expenditure on marketing to be demonstrated by bills from external suppliers. The society can also ask for a costed proposal and insist that it is involved in deciding how an agreed sum is spent. It is not uncommon for societies to ask that they should check all promotional copy but this should not be too rigid a requirement as it is not always possible to arrange such checking without losing a sales opportunity. In all these cases there is an element of trust within an overall structure that is totally clear on the main points.

9.4.14 Legal questions

Finally there are a number of areas where there are legal principles involved. Obviously some of these depend on the legal jurisdiction. Societies in all jurisdictions are urged to insist upon copyright in their name for all their publications and a precise definition of what rights are actually given to the partner. Many legal clauses relate to what happens if either party terminates the contract. There should be arrangements for the return of rights to the society in the case of books or cancellation of the contract in the case of series or journals. If the publishing partner allows a book to go out of print and has not reprinted within a reasonable time, all rights should revert to the society. The delay should normally be defined: one year is the absolute maximum. In all cases if the partner fails to comply with the terms of the agreement, particularly the financial terms where non-payment is easy to show, the contract is automatically cancelled if action does not follow a specified period following a warning. A similar cancellation should obtain if the publisher goes into liquidation, except for what is called "the purposes of reconstruction" under English law. Some societies, in view of the number of mergers and take-overs in the present climate, may wish to insist that the contract be not automatically transferred to a new owner. If the publisher does not contract directly with the editor of a journal or of a book series and this is left in the hands of the society, the partner may ask the society concerned to give warranties that the work is its own and free from libel. This is a reasonable request but the society may wish to take out insurance in case its assurances turn out to be ill-founded. Societies should make sure that the termination clauses in any contract are clear and understood by both parties. They are often drawn up badly. The starting date of a contract should be defined closely. In the case of a journal does it start with the first issue, with the beginning of the year or at the time of signature and does it end at so many years after that date or at the end of the year in question? It is important that societies should take note of the termination date, especially if there is automatic renewal, and should take the opportunity to review the relationship.

9.5   Arrangements over electronic publishing

The potential represented by the Internet for improved communication of science has been set out in chapter 3. There is constant change and it is often the case that contracts between a society and a partner do not cover all possibilities. Societies have in some cases lagged behind commercial publishers in taking advantage of this potential. It is preferable that societies choose their partner because they want to expand the penetration of their publications and give the partner scope to do so. The best way to express this recommended type of relationship contractually is in terms of the different functions (production, marketing and so forth) listed in 9.4 above. If the publishing partner is to be the Internet host (see 3.4), as is likely to be the case, the contract will specify in technical detail obligations and warranties relating to this particular relationship.

CHAPTER 10
COMMUNICATING SCIENCE WORLDWIDE

10.1 The mission of ICSU

Like other scientific organisations, publishing houses and academic institutions, ICSU has for some time donated copies of books and journals to institutions in developing countries, and has encouraged members of the ICSU family to do the same. However, although such contributions are worthwhile and very much welcomed by recipients, it was recognised that the dearth of scientific literature in many regions of the world was so severe that a more comprehensive and global approach was needed.

10.2 The foundation of INASP

Hence in 1992 ICSU Press, in co-operation with UNESCO and the Third World Academy of Sciences and with assistance from the European Community, established the International Network for the Availability of Scientific Publications (INASP). INASP is a co-operative network of partners whose aim is to improve world-wide access to information. In particular its mission is to improve the flow of information within and between countries, especially those with less developed systems of publication.

10.3 The objectives of INASP

The objectives of INASP are:

- To map, support and strengthen existing programmes involved in the distribution, local publication, access and exchange of books, journals and related material (e.g. maps and charts, audio-visual materials, software and CD-ROM).

- To encourage, and support new initiatives that will increase local publication and general access to high-quality scientific literature.

- To identify methods that will permit the ongoing and sustainable distribution of scientific publications.

10.4   Information about INASP

10.4.1 How to find out more

Details of the targeted programmes and activities by means of which INASP works towards these goals and relevant publications (some of them available free of charge) can be obtained from the secretariat at 27 Park End Street, Oxford OX1 1HU, United Kingdom. The telephone number of INASP is +44 1865 24909, the fax is +44 1865 251060 and the e-mail address is inasp@gn.apc.org. However the INASP website provides by far the best way of tapping what is offered and in particular mention should be made of a new feature INASP LINKS & RESOURCES – "Access to Information" which points to relevant sources on the Internet. The URL for INASP is http://oneworld.org/inasp/. Many of the topics examined in these Guidelines are given more specific treatment in INASP publications and, as the organisation is constantly adding items to what it has available, regular consultation of the website is recommended.

10.4.2 How to find out about other initiatives associated with INASP

As mentioned in chapter 3, there are initiatives by a number of organisations as well as to foster electronic journals INASP (see the INASP website for African Journals On-Line). One such organisation is Bioline Publications and its associated Electronic Publishing Trust for Development (see the following websites: www.bdt.org.br/bioline/ and dspace.dial.pipex.com/bioline/). Another is ExtraMED which produces 10 CDROMs a year containing the full page images of nearly 3000 medical and health science journals from developing countries and promotes them to libraries world-wide: for further information email 100060.172@compuserve.com. The Open Society Institute runs

GUIDELINES FOR SCIENTIFIC PUBLISHING

the Center for Publishing Development in Budapest (www.osi.hu/cpd) which helps to develop local publishing initiatives in Eastern Europe. Another relevant site of the same organisation is www.oneworld.org.

10.5   Training courses

There are a number of training courses which are available to staff at publishing houses throughout the world. Some are run by government organisations such as the British Council and some by scientific organisations such as the American Association for the Advancement of Science (AAAS). INASP is also able to advise on how to access such courses and whether they are likely to be appropriate to individual needs.

APPENDIX 1
ADVICE TO THE SCIENTIFIC AUTHOR

This short appendix for authors is intended to complement the rest of these Guidelines intended for the learned society as a publisher

Understanding your own needs.

It is possible to publish your own book or even your own journal but you are not advised to do so. Very few attempts to do so are successful and although, in the online environment, putting information on the web is easy and delivery is very much easier than in the print environment, publications which are not validated by a publisher do not usually carry the same sort of credibility. In addition, in the print world most publishing functions are time-consuming, uncreative and frankly boring. These guidelines are not concerned with making money for the author. If you think your book is likely to be a best-seller you should not go to a learned society for reasons set out in section 2.3. Publication with a learned society ensures the stamp of approval of your peers combined with the best penetration of your ideas to your chosen audience.

Choosing a publisher

Your choice of a publisher will depend on whom you are trying to reach. Some learned societies are not geared to reaching the international audience. You may wish to edit a journal: in this case take your idea to a publisher with a journals list. Much of the advice in chapter 9 about choosing a partner is relevant here. It is important to make yourself aware of the policies of the publisher you intend to use. It is not unreasonable to demand from a publisher in writing a clear statement of their pricing policies and specifically their intentions relating to your book or journal before committing yourself.

Exercising your rights

Scientists are urged to look closely at the guidance on copyright in chapter 3, which represents the policies of major learned societies and the current position of ICSU. You may wish to retain your copyright and offer to grant publishing rights instead. You are advised to check that the publisher concerned is actually using the rights you are asked to grant. You may also wish to reserve the right to put a journal article, after review and acceptance, on your own open website. Some publishers will not agree but many will if specifically asked the question. Whatever the decision you may make it is important to remember that whatever you write is your intellectual property unless you have signed a document or accepted a contract giving it away.

Getting help

These Guidelines are part of the service provided by ICSU Press. It is part of their remit to help the individual scientist as well as the corporate members of the ICSU family. Mention has also been made of INASP and what it offers in chapter 10.

APPENDIX 2
A CONTRACT WITH A JOURNAL EDITOR

Please read the warnings in 4.1.6 before looking at this sample document. Note also that the sections in italics are either optional or present alternatives

The contract starts here:

AGREEMENT

(1)   *<Name and Address >*("the Editor")

and

(2)   *<LEGAL NAME OF PUBLISHER OR SOCIETY WITH ADDRESS>, <Imprint if different>*("the Publisher")

This Agreement sets out the terms and conditions for your editing of the Journal entitled *<Title>* ("the Journal") *[the aims and scope of which are set out in the attached Schedule 1]*:

1.   Term of Agreement

1.1   This Agreement shall *[commence on <date>/ the date when this Agreement is signed by the Editor and]*continue, unless terminated under clause 1.2 below, until 31 December *[<year>]* and thereafter for consecutive three-year periods unless and until terminated by either party on giving at least six months written notice to expire on 31 December *[<year>]*, or on the expiry date of any subsequent three year period.

1.2   The Publisher may terminate the Agreement at any time between *[<date>]* and *[<date>]* on giving six months written notice to the Editor, if in the opinion of the Publisher at its sole discretion either (i) the revenue accruing to the Journal is insufficient to project financial viability within a reasonable period of time; or (ii) the Editor, for any reason and notwithstanding the provisions of any other clause in this Agreement, is unable or unsuitable to fulfil the duties set out in clause 4 of this Agreement.

2.   Ownership

2.1   The Publisher and its successors and assigns is and shall remain the sole owner of the Journal, including without limitation the goodwill and copyright (if any) in the title *[<title>]*, and the copyright and all rights of the nature of copyright in and to the layout, compilation, typography and all editorial and illustrative material to be published in the Journal.

2.2   The Editor hereby assigns to the Publisher copyright and all rights of the nature of copyright in any editorial or illustrative material published in the Journal, which may or may not include corrections and amendments to the contributions, and written or created by the Editor ("the Editorial Material") to which the Editor is now or may at any time be entitled, and the Editor shall sign and execute all such documents and deeds as may reasonably be required in order to perfect, protect or enforce any of the rights assigned under this Agreement.

2.3   The Publisher shall be the sole owner of the physical inventory of all issues of the Journal it publishes either in print or other forms and the plates, film, dies and similar items used in the production of such issues.

2.4   The Editor shall secure, prior to submission of the relevant contribution to the Publisher, signed agreements with each contributor in a form prescribed in writing from time to time by the Publisher in respect of each contribution to be accepted for the Journal by the Editor and shall submit the signed agreement with each submission, including with that the agreement that all permissions which the contributor is obliged to obtain in accordance with the requirements of clauses 2.5 and 2.6 below.

2.5   If copyright material is to be included in the Journal, the Editor shall require contributors to secure, at their expense, from the copyright owner written permission in a form which will be specified by the Publisher for the reproduction of such material in the Journal.

2.6   If photographs of patients are to be included in the Journal, the Editor shall require contributors to gain permission from the patient in a form which shall be specified by the Publisher or establish that such permission as specified by the Publisher has been gained by the copyright holder.

2.7   The Publisher shall own the list of subscribers to the Journal and the copyright and all rights to and in such a list.

3.   Publisher's responsibility

The Publisher shall be responsible at its sole discretion for the production and manufacturing, pricing, fulfilment, mailing, customer service and promotion of the Journal and all other business aspects of the publication of the Journal.

4.   Editor's responsibilities

4.1   The Editor shall have the full responsibility for determining the editorial content of the Journal which shall be to a standard and of a nature determined at the sole discretion of the Publisher after consultation with the Editor.

4.2   The Editor shall arrange for peer-review of contributions to the Journal and shall make the final selection of contributions published in the Journal after consultation with the Publisher.

4.3   Notwithstanding the above clauses 4.1 and 4.2, the Publisher reserves the right to refuse to publish any contribution which, in the view of the Publisher, is defamatory or otherwise an infringement under the terms of the warranty by the Editor in clause 18 of this Agreement.

4.4 Notwithstanding the above clauses 4.1 and 4.2 the Publisher reserves the right to refuse to publish any contribution not covered by the form of agreement described in clause 2.4 above or not accompanied, where necessary, by the written evidence that relevant permissions as described in clauses 2.5 and 2.6 have been gained to cover material to be reproduced in the contribution.

4.5 The Editor shall prepare any Editorial Material as shall be customarily published in the Journal or shall be required by the Publisher.

4.6 The Editor shall collect in a form specified by the Publisher such information relating to the dates of submission of contributions to the Journal and the decision to reject, revise or accept the said contributions as the Publisher shall require and deliver the said information to the Publisher on a regular basis in accordance with a timetable notified by the Publisher.

5. Editorial structure

The Editor shall be assisted in performing the obligations of the Editor by such associate editors and editorial board members as are agreed in writing by the Publisher. The Publisher may enter into a written agreement with each person so engaged in assisting in the editing and preparation of the Journal on terms to be determined by the Publisher at its sole discretion.

6. Publication procedures

6.1 The Editor shall submit to the Publisher, in accordance with a schedule which the Publisher shall agree in writing with the Editor, an appropriate number of pages of finished and accepted editorial and illustrative material to make an issue as set out in clause 7 below. This material shall be typewritten or produced using a word-processor, single-sided with reasonable margins, double-spaced, with references at the end prepared according to the Publisher's requirements, and illustrations separately prepared and in a form which can be used and keyed into the text, or preferably on a diskette with a hard copy prepared as described above. The Editor shall submit such material in the English language after it has been peer-reviewed and reviewed by the Editor for content, style, form, conciseness, clarity and scientific accuracy.

6.2   The Publisher shall copy-edit and mark for the typesetter all materials submitted under clause 6.1, and shall transmit the copy-edited materials to the typesetter. Copy-editing includes, but is not limited to a review of proper punctuation, sentence construction, clarity of communication in the contribution concerned, conformity to Journal style (such style being as agreed between the Publisher and the Editor), and also the sizing of illustrations and such markings as shall be needed for the typesetter.

6.3   The Publisher shall transmit proofs to the Editor and where appropriate after consultation with the Editor, directly to the relevant contributors at addresses furnished by the Editor, and shall see the materials through to published form with minimal further attention from the Editor provided that, if there is disagreement between the Publisher and the contributor about alterations made by the copy-editor, the Publisher may require the Editor to take responsibility for the published form of the material in accordance with clause 4.1 above of this Agreement.

7.   Publication schedule and format

7.1   The Publisher intends to publish a volume comprising [*<number>*] issues of the Journal in [*<year>*] [*in the months of <list months>*]. The Publisher shall make available a total of [*<number>*] pages of editorial and illustrative matter for that volume.

7.2   The aggregate number of pages in any one volume may be distributed unequally over the numbered issues but the number of pages in each issue must be a multiple of sixteen pages.

7.3   The Publisher may increase or decrease the frequency of publication of the Journal or the annual page budget in subsequent years at its sole discretion after consultation with the Editor.

7.4   The size, format, cover and title page designs, paper weight and quality and other production particulars shall be determined at the sole discretion of the Publisher.

7.5   The Publisher may permit additional pages in any volume of the Journal provided that the extra costs of reproducing and distributing such pages as determined by the Publisher is borne by a third party found by the Editor or the Publisher.

7.6   *[The Publisher shall, at its cost and expense, reproduce black-and-white illustrations in the Journal in a manner substantially equivalent to the reproduction of similar illustrations in competing or relevant journals. The Editor may accept four-colour illustrations if the colour is relevant to the editorial aims of the contribution but the Publisher will ask the Editor to make the acceptance of such illustrations contingent on the contributor reimbursing the Publisher to cover the costs of the inclusion of the illustration in the Journal in accordance with a scale of charges which shall be drawn up by the Publisher and notified in writing to the Editor from time to time].*

8.   Page charges and offprints

8.1   The Publisher shall set no page charges or submission charges for contributions to the Journal in *[<year>]*, other than such charges as shall be levied for sponsored issues or sponsored sections of issues as referred to in clause 7.5 above, but the Publisher shall decide policy in this matter in subsequent years at its sole discretion after consultation with the Editor. *[The Publisher shall set page charges/submission charges for contributions to the Journal which shall in <year> be as set out in schedule <number> attached to this Agreement and shall decide policy in this matter including the determination of charges to be levied in subsequent years at its sole discretion after consultation with the Editor].*

8.2   In accordance with the policies of the Publisher, offprints will be made available to contributors at a scale of charges to be determined at the sole discretion of the Publisher subject to payment being made by contributors in accordance with a schedule drawn up by the Publisher and made known in a timely manner to the contributors. If the contributor is unable to furnish an order or make payment in time for offprints to be made up, the Publisher may offer reprints to the contributor in accordance with a scale determined by the Publisher .

8.3   Offprints or reprints of material published in the Journal may also be sold to parties other than the authors of the material.

9. Sales and subscriptions

9.1   The Publisher shall determine the subscription rates and the terms of sale of the Journal throughout the world at its sole discretion.

9.2   The Publisher shall, at its own expense, promote the sale of subscriptions to the Journal throughout the world.

9.3   The Publisher may seek special arrangements with or sponsorship by appropriate learned or professional bodies in order to increase the exposure of the Journal by offering special subscription rates; such arrangements or sponsorships may involve representation for the body concerned in the editorial structure of the Journal.

9.4   The Publisher may seek special arrangements with or sponsorship by pharmaceutical companies and other commercial organizations in order to increase the exposure of the Journal by offering special subscription rates.

10. Advertising and supplements

10.1   The Publisher shall be responsible for soliciting and obtaining advertising material for publication in the Journal and shall set the advertising rates for the Journal.

10.2 The Publisher shall consult with the Editor, where practicable, concerning the appropriateness of all new advertising material but a final decision on inclusion in the Journal shall be at the sole discretion of the Publisher.

10.3 The Publisher shall insert in each issue of the Journal containing advertising material a disclaimer that the publication of advertising in the Journal does not constitute on the part of the Publisher or the Editor any guarantee or endorsement of the quality or value of the advertised products or services or of the claims made for such products by their respective advertisers.

10.4 *[The Publisher may not place advertising matter within the editorial or illustrative matter included in the Journal without the prior written consent of the Editor].*

10.5 The Publisher may publish sponsored supplements to the Journal at its sole discretion *[after consultation with and review by the Editor].*

11. Editor's remuneration

[The Publisher shall pay to the Editor, to an address or account nominated by the Editor [immediately/ divided into <number> equal parts and paid by the end of <months>/on <date>] following the signature of this Agreement, a fee of <amount specifying currency> for <year> and the same amount on the same dates on years subsequent while the Agreement is in force.].

12. Expenses

[The publisher shall reimburse the Editor not exceeding <amount> in <year> payable in <number> equal instalments on or about the first day of <list months> and the same amounts on the same dates in years subsequent while the Agreement is in force subject to the production of vouchers or other satisfactory documentary evidence. No expenses will be paid in respect of any expenses incurred after the termination of this Agreement].

13. Stationery

The Publisher will make available to the Editor letterheads, and other stationery pertaining to the Journal, to be designed at the sole discretion of the Publisher after consultation with the Editor.

14. Editorial copies

The Publisher shall provide the Editor with five free copies of each issue of the Journal published during the term of this Agreement for the Editor's personal use and not for resale.

15. Termination

15.1 Should this Agreement be terminated for whatever reason under the terms of clause 1 above of the Agreement, the Editor shall within thirty days deliver to the Publisher both the originals or copies of all files relating to the editorial and illustrative matter for the Journal, including correspondence, and unpublished editorial material, manuscript or proofs which may be in the Editor's possession at the time.

15.2 Should the Editor cease to be editor of the Journal, but subsequently receive submissions to the Journal or correspondence relating to the Journal, such material shall be passed to the Publisher or as instructed by the Publisher not more than thirty days after the date of receipt of such material.

15.3 The editor shall not within one year of the termination of this Agreement act as an editor of another journal with similar aims and scope to <title> for another publisher unless this termination is consequent on the sale or assignment of the Journal to another publisher.

16.   Force majeure

If this Agreement cannot be performed or its obligations fulfilled for any reason beyond the reasonable control of either party that party shall give to the other written notice of the inability stating the reason in question. The operation of this Agreement shall be suspended during the period in which such reason continues. If the reason continues for a period of more than thirty days the party not claiming relief under this clause shall have the right to terminate this Agreement forthwith upon giving written notice to the other part.

17.   Tax liabilities

[It is declared that it is the intention of the parties that the Editor shall be responsible for all income tax liability and National Insurance or similar contributions in respect of the fees payable under this Agreement and the Editor undertakes to indemnify the Publisher in respect of any claims that may be made against the Publisher in respect of income tax or National Insurance or similar contributions relating to the Editor's services under this Agreement].

18.   Editor's warranties

18.1   The Editor hereby warrants to the Publisher that:

i)   The Editor has full power to make this Agreement and is the sole owner of the rights to be assigned by the Editor under this Agreement.

ii)   The Editorial Material is original to the Editor

iii)   The Editorial Material has not previously been published in any form .

iv)   The Editor has not assigned or licensed or otherwise disposed of any rights of copyright or any other rights in or to the Editorial Material except under this Agreement.

86

v) The Editorial Material is not a violation or infringement of any existing copyright or right of any third party, does not contain anything defamatory, obscene, blasphemous or otherwise unlawful.

vi) So far as the Editor is aware the Journal does not contain any statements purporting to be facts that are inaccurate or untrue.

18.2 All warranties shall survive the termination of this Agreement.

19. Warranties and representations of the Publisher

19.1 The Publisher represents and warrants that it has the right and power to enter into and to perform in accordance with the Agreement, and that the persons executing this Agreement on its behalf are authorized to do so.

19.2 The Publisher shall give to the Editor prompt notice of any claim arising against the Journal, the Publisher or the Editor or any action that may constitute a breach of any warranty to the Editor contained in clause 18 of this Agreement, and the Editor, if they choose, may participate in the defence against any such claim with counsel of their own choosing and at their own expense.

20. Notices

Any notice pursuant to the Agreement shall be in writing and shall be delivered, in person, by prepaid commercial messenger, Express Mail or other means providing expedited delivery, a means of being traced and a return receipt confirming delivery, and addressed as follows:

20.1 The Editor

<name and address>

or to such other address or person as the Editor may designate by written notice.

20.2 The Publisher

<name and address>

or to such other address or person as the Publisher may designate by written notice. Notices shall be deemed given on the tenth business day after mailing.

21. Assignment

The Publisher may assign this Agreement or any interest herein to any person or legal entity. The Editor may assign only the Editor's right to receive any amounts payable after receipt by the Publisher of written notice of such assignment.

22. Value Added Tax

[All sums payable to the Editor under this Agreement are exclusive of Value Added Tax ("VAT") which shall where applicable be payable in addition at the rate in force at the time for payment subject to the Editor informing the Publisher of the Editor's VAT registration number in order that the Publisher can operate a self-billing system for VAT. The Editor shall immediately advise the Publisher should the VAT status or number of the Editor change].

23 Headings

The headings in this Agreement shall not affect its interpretation and are for convenience only.

24. Complete Agreement

This Agreement constitutes the complete understanding of the parties as to the Journal and no representation other than is contained herein shall be binding on either party. No alteration, modification or waiver of any provision shall be valid unless in writing and signed by all parties hereto.

25. Governing law

[This Agreement shall be governed by and construed under English law and any dispute or difference between the parties which cannot be amicably resolved shall be subject to the non-exclusive jurisdiction of the English courts].

AS WITNESS

The parties have executed this Agreement on the date first set forth above.

By..Date.................................

<name>
Editor

By..Date ....

<name>
<official title>

APPENDIX 3
COPYRIGHT TRANSFER OF JOURNAL ARTICLES

This contract was written for use under English law. It is one of a group of contracts which allow for different eventualities allowing for licensing (grant) of publishing rights rather than the transfer of copyright, signature by an employer rather than the author and also warranties for those such as certain government employees who have no copyright to transfer. Some publishers allow for all these eventualities in one form using boxes for options. The procedural arrangements that form part of this document are worth considering closely. It is important to all publishers that they have been given the rights to publish and that they do their best to make sure that the documents granting those rights are signed and returned promptly. Note also that the rights "given back" are in a state of flux. Currently most publishers do not explicitly grant back the right to put up an accepted article on an open (as distinct from a secure) website but this situation appears to be changing. It is possible to prepare a document to cover the publication of journal articles under the terms of which the author retains rights and grants only specific rights to the publisher.

The form starts here:

Please return a signed copy of this form as soon as possible to <<*name of person*>> at <<*name and address of publisher*>>. The article cannot be published until this signed document is received. A fax to <<*number*>> is acceptable but the original must follow.

<< *NAME AND IMPRINT OF PUBLISHER* >> COPYRIGHT TRANSFER FORM

In order that << *Name and imprint of publisher* >> can make available your work to the fullest extent both directly and through intermediaries and in both print and electronic form, the transfer of the copyright in this article has to be explicitly stated.

Article entitled :

Name(s) of Author(s) :

Title of Journal :

I acknowledge that any copyright and all other rights of whatever nature subsisting attached to the material described above ("the Article") prepared by me/us shall belong to << *Name and imprint of publisher* >> ("the Publisher"). I hereby assign to the Publisher the entire copyright and all other rights of whatever nature in and to the Article in all languages and in all media to which I am now and may in the future be entitled throughout the world for the full period of copyright and all renewals and extensions.

I warrant that the Article has not been published before, and that I have obtained permission from the copyright holder to reproduce in the Article in all media material not owned by me, that the Article does not contain any unlawful statements, and that it does not infringe any rights of others.

Notwithstanding the above the Publisher confirms that the Author retains all proprietary rights other than copyright such as patent rights and shall identify the Author(s) as the author(s) of the Article and shall not alter the text of the published article without the agreement of the Author (s).

The Publisher grants back to the Author the following rights:

> To make copies of all or part of the Work for personal use including use in presentations, the Author's use in classroom teaching, and for the personal use of colleagues providing that the copies are not offered for sale or distributed in a systematic way outside the employing institution.

> To make copies of the Work for internal distribution within the institution which employs the Author.

To use after publication all or part of the Work in a book by the Author or in a collection of the Author's work.

To use figures and tables from the Work, and up to 250 words of text, for any purpose.

Signed :   Dated :

IMPORTANT : All authors must sign or a valid power of attorney must be produced authorising a signatory to sign on behalf of an author.

If the ownership of copyright in this Article is in the hands of your employer, or the Article is written by an employee of the US government, please get in touch with us at once and we shall send you an appropriate form which we shall need signed and returned before we can publish your contribution.

APPENDIX 4
A FORM FOR SEEKING PERMISSION TO USE COPYRIGHTED MATERIAL.

This form was devised for use under the law of England and may not be appropriate for use in other jurisdictions.

The form starts here:

< NAME OF PUBLISHER> Permission Request Form

Important: Authors applying for permission, make sure you fully complete both boxes below and, if possible, attach a photocopy of the material you wish to use. Once you have obtained all permission clearances from copyright holders, please return all permission forms and any related documents together with your manuscript to your publishing editor at < Name of Publisher>

To copyright holders, kindly return permission clearance to <u>the author</u> at the address below.

To (copyright holder):

....

....

....

....

From (author of new work):

....

....

....

....

New Work

Title:

Author/Editor:

Contributor's name:

Chapter title & number/article title:

Figure number(s):

Figure Legend(s):

Source Work

Title of book/journal:

If journal, give volume number and title of article:

Date of Publication:

Author(s):

Figure/plate number(s) or details of material concerned and page number(s):

We are preparing a new work for publication in which we wish to reproduce material (illustration(s)/text), details of which are given above. We would be grateful if you could grant us the non-exclusive right to reproduce the material and, if necessary, to redraw or modify the material for use in this edition and all subsequent editions, revisions and translations of the work and in derivative versions based on the work, in all print and non-print formats and media for distribution throughout the world, including distribution through document delivery services and inclusion in photocopying licensing schemes (e.g. the Publishers Licensing Society in the UK and the Copyright Clearance Center in the USA).

If you do not hold the copyright in this material please indicate below to whom our request should be referred. If the permission of the author is also required, kindly supply current address details.

Where images of patients are required for use in a medical work, please provide proof of patient consent, or details of whom to contact to obtain consent.

Yours faithfully

....
(Author)

AUTHORIZATION

(either)

I/we hereby grant permission for the above material to be reproduced by you and your licensees in all media and in any languages (as requested above) in your forthcoming publication, either:

(a)   with the usual acknowledgement, or
(b)   provided that the acknowledgement includes
         reference to:

I/we confirm that I hold the necessary rights and that no consent is required of any third party to grant such permission.

Signature: ....

For: .... Date: ....

(or)

We do not hold the rights to this material. Requests for permission to reproduce this material should be addressed to:

Name: ....

Address: ....

....

....

....